Mark Ibbotson
Bryan Stephens

Business
START-UP 1

Student's Book

CAMBRIDGE
UNIVERSITY PRESS

D1205310

CAMBRIDGE
UNIVERSITY PRESS

University Printing House, Cambridge CB2 8BS, United Kingdom

Cambridge University Press is part of the University of Cambridge.

It furthers the University's mission by disseminating knowledge in the pursuit of education, learning and research at the highest international levels of excellence.

www.cambridge.org
Information on this title: www.cambridge.org/9780521534659

© Cambridge University Press 2006

This publication is in copyright. Subject to statutory exception and to the provisions of relevant collective licensing agreements, no reproduction of any part may take place without the written permission of Cambridge University Press.

First published 2006
14th printing 2015

Printed in Italy by Rotolito Lombarda S.p.A.

A catalogue record for this publication is available from the British Library

ISBN 978-0-521-53465-9 Student's Book
ISBN 978-0-521-67207-8 Workbook with CD-ROM / Audio CD
ISBN 978-0-521-53466-6 Teacher's Book
ISBN 978-0-521-53467-3 Audio Cassettes (2)
ISBN 978-0-521-53468-0 Audio CDs (2)
ISBN 978-3-12-539763-7 Student's Book Klett Version

Cambridge University Press has no responsibility for the persistence or accuracy of URLs for external or third-party internet websites referred to in this publication, and does not guarantee that any content on such websites is, or will remain, accurate or appropriate. Information regarding prices, travel timetables and other factual information given in this work is correct at the time of first printing but Cambridge University Press does not guarantee the accuracy of such information thereafter.

Contents

1 Welcome

1.1 Meeting people

GRAMMAR *be*: present simple

VOCABULARY Introductions   Alphabet A–Z

1 a ▶▶ **1** Listen to Joe and Claire meeting at the offices of ZY.

Claire Hello, I'm Claire Martin.
Joe   Hi, I'm Joe Kent. Nice to meet you.
Claire Nice to meet you.
Joe   Welcome to ZY Systems.
Claire Thanks.

b Practise the conversation in pairs. Change roles.

c ▶▶ **2** Listen and fill in the gaps.

nice   hi   I'm   thanks   welcome

Ian   Hello. ¹ *I'm* Ian Field.
Sally   ² .... I'm Sally Winters.
Ian   ³ .... to meet you, Sally. ⁴ ....
        to New York.
Sally   ⁵ ....

d Vocabulary practice ···> Page 94, Exercise 1.

2 a ▶▶ **3** PRONUNCIATION Say the alphabet. Listen and repeat.

A B C D E F G H I J K L M
N O P Q R S T U V W X Y Z

b Work with a partner. Student A says a letter. Student B points to it. Take it in turns.

c Which letters have the same sounds? Fill in the chart.

/eɪ/	/iː/	/e/	/aɪ/	/juː/
A	**B**	**F**	**I**	**Q**
H	C	L	Y	U

d ▶▶ **4** Listen. Put the companies in the order you hear them. Write 1–10 in the boxes.

☐   ☐

☐ **IBM**

☐1   ☐

☐   ☐ GEC

☐ *JFK Cargo*

☐ AOL   ☐ RNX Auto

e ▶▶| 4 **Listen again. Practise saying the company names.**

f Think of more companies that use letters for their names. Student A says the companies and Student B writes them. Change roles.

3 a ▶▶| 5 **Listen to Joe introducing Claire to the team at ZY. Fill in the gaps.**

I'm you're he's she's we're they're

Joe	Hello everyone. This is Claire Martin. ¹ _She's_ from IBM. Claire, this is Paul Sampson. ² _____ from ZY Communications.
Paul	Hello Claire.
Joe	And this is Anne Pol and David Tarn. ³ _____ from ZY Design.
David	Nice to meet you.
Anne	Hello.
Sam	And ⁴ _____ Sam Pick and this is Lara Kay. ⁵ _____ from ZY Holdings. So, ⁶ _____ from New York, Claire?
Claire	Yes. Nice to meet you, everyone.

be	
I am (I'm)	you are (you're)
he is (he's)	she is (she's)
we are (we're)	they are (they're)

···> **Grammar reference 1**

b Grammar practice ···> Page 94, Exercise 2.

c Practise introductions. Use the photos.
This is ... . He's/She's from ... .

4 Communication practice 1 ···> Page 78. Work in groups of three.

5 Meet other students in the group and introduce students.
Hello/Hi. I'm ... . Nice to meet you.
This is ... . He's/She's from ... .

USEFUL LANGUAGE
Hello/Hi.
Nice to meet you.
Welcome to ... .
Thanks.
I'm Sue Taylor. I'm from TP Software.
This is Peter Elton. He's from LMS.

Paul Sampson – ZY Communications

Lara Kay – ZY Holdings

Sam Pick – ZY Holdings

Anne Pol – ZY Design

David Tarn – ZY Design

Questions with where and be

Where are you/they from?
Where's he/she from?
(Where's = Where is)

Are you from London?
Is he from London?

···> **Grammar reference 1 and 8**

d Grammar practice ···> Page 94, Exercise 3.

2 a Work with a partner. Can you guess where the people are from?

1	Brad Carrington	a	Brazil
2	Hans Schwartz	b	China
3	Jan Grabowski	c	France
4	Maria Gonzales	d	Germany
5	Shen Lin	e	Poland
6	Nathalie Lemaire	f	Spain
7	Pedro da Silva	g	the UK
8	Alison Smith	h	the USA

1 a ▶▶ **6** Listen to the conversation. Fill in the gaps.

from he OK right you

David So, where are you ¹ *from* , Claire?
Claire New York.
David ² _____ . The Big Apple!
Claire Yes! And you, David? Are ³ _____ from Paris?
David No, I'm from Lille. ZY Design, in Lille.
Claire ⁴ _____ . And where's Paul from? Is ⁵ _____ from London?
David Yes.

b Practise the conversation in pairs.

c Answer the questions.
1 Where's David from? *He's from Lille*
2 Where's Paul from? _____
3 Where's Claire from? _____
4 Where are you from? _____

b ▶▶ **7** Listen and check your answers.

c Work with a partner. Take it in turns to ask questions about the people in 2a.
A Where's Brad Carrington from?
B He's from the USA.

d ▶▶ **8** PRONUNCIATION Listen to the countries in 2a. Write them in the chart.

O	Oo	Ooo	oO	oOO	oOOO
			Brazil		

3 **a** **Where are the cities? Fill in the gaps.**

north   south   east   west   centre

1 Toulon is **in the** ....*south*.... **of** France, **near** Marseille.
2 Madrid is **in the** .... **of** Spain.
3 Beijing is **in the** ....-................ **of** China.
4 Chester is **in the** .... **of** the UK, **near** Manchester.

FRANCE

Marseille

Toulon

Madrid

SPAIN

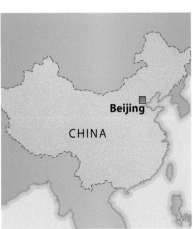

Beijing

CHINA

Manchester

Chester

UK

4 Communication practice 2 ···⟩
Page 78. Work with a partner.

5 **a** **Do any cities or regions in your country have a different name or pronunciation in English? Write and say their English names.**

b **Talk to other students in the group. Find out where they're from.**

USEFUL LANGUAGE

I'm from Macau.
Macau? Where's that?
It's in China, near Hong Kong.

Where are you from?
I'm from Bremen, in the north of Germany.

Countries
Brazil   China   France   Germany
Poland   Spain   the UK   the USA

b ▶▶ **9** **Listen and check your answers.**

c Vocabulary practice ···⟩ Page 94, Exercise 4.

d **Ask questions about cities in your country or in other countries. Test your partner!**

A Where's ... ?
B It's in the north/south/east/west of ... (near ...).

e **Work with a partner. Student A chooses a city from 3a. Student B asks questions. Take it in turns.**

A Where are you from?
B Toulon.
A Toulon? Where's that?
B It's in the south of France, near Marseille.

1.3	Offering and asking for drinks	GRAMMAR	*a/an*
		VOCABULARY	Drinks

1 **a** **Write the drinks (a–f) under the pictures on the menu.**

> a apple juice   b coffee   c iced tea   d mineral water   e orange juice   f tea

1 _____coffee_____

2 _____

3 _____

4 _____

5 _____

6 _____

b **PRONUNCIATION Put the drinks under the correct stress marks.**

1 Oo	o	4 o	o
apple	_juice_	_____	_____
2 Oo	o	5 Oo	
_____	_____	_____	
3 Ooo	Oo	6 o	
_____	_____	_____	

c ▶▶ **10** Now listen to six people. What drinks (a–f) from 1a do they ask for?

1 [b]   2 ☐   3 ☐   4 ☐
5 ☐   6 ☐

d ▶▶ **10** Listen again. Write the drinks in the chart.

	Drinks		
a	*coffee*		
an			

---

a/an

*Use **a** before consonants:* **a** <u>c</u>offee
*Use **an** before vowels:* **an** <u>o</u>range juice

···> Grammar reference 4

e Grammar practice ···> Page 94, Exercise 5.

2 **a** ▶▶ **11** Listen to the conversation. Fill in the gaps.

Joe ¹ *Would* you like a drink, Claire?

Claire ² _____ , please. Could I have a tea?

Joe Yes. Milk? Sugar?

Claire With milk, ³_____ . No sugar.

Joe OK. And Anne?

Anne ⁴_____ I have an orange juice, please?

Joe Sure.

b ▶▶ **12** PRONUNCIATION How do you say *a* and *an* in these sentences? Listen and repeat.

1 Could I have a coffee, please?
　　　　　　　/ə/

2 Could I have an orange juice?
　　　　　　　/ən/

c Practise saying the sentences.

d Vocabulary practice ···> Page 94, Exercise 6.

3 Communication practice 3 ···> Page 78. Work with a partner.

4 **a** How many drinks do you know in English? Write them in the chart.

Drinks
orange juice
mineral water

b What's your favourite drink? Ask other students.

USEFUL LANGUAGE

Would you like a drink?
Yes, please. / No, thanks.
Could I have a/an ..., please?
Yes. / Sure.
Milk? Sugar?
With milk, please.
No sugar.

Drinks
coffee　tea　(mineral) water
orange juice　apple juice　iced tea
Note: Mineral water *can be* still *or* sparkling.
Could I have mineral water, please?
Still or sparkling?

---

2 Numbers

2.1 Telephone numbers and email addresses

GRAMMAR What's ...? – It's ... . *my* and *your*

VOCABULARY Numbers 0–10   Email addresses

1 a ▶▶ 13 Listen and repeat the numbers.

0   1   2   3   4   5
6   7   8   9   10

b Write the numbers in the correct boxes.

eight	five	four	nine	one	seven
six	three	two	zero/oh		

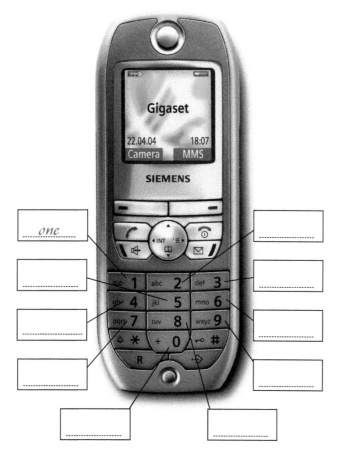

one

2 a ▶▶ 14 Listen to four conversations. Complete the telephone numbers.

(1)

0 28 6 10 _____ _____ 93

(2)

JFK Cargo
TEL: _____ 12 _____ 37 4 _____ 59

(3)

Panorama | Consulting

Susan Taylor

Tel: 0 _____ 632 7 _____ 49 _____ _____

(4)

PAUL WEBB
☎
07 _____ 8 2 _____ 137 _____ 6

b Practise saying the telephone numbers in 2a.

c ▶▶ 15 PRONUNCIATION Listen and repeat. Then practise the conversations in pairs.

1 **A** What's your number?

   B My phone number?

   A Yes.

2 **A** My phone number's two one two ...

   B Sorry?

   A T w o   o n e   t w o ...

3 **A** Five eight?

   B No, <u>nine</u> eight.

   A Right.

4 **A** <u>So</u>, two one two, six three seven, four eight five nine.

   B That's right.

Questions with **what;** **my** *and* **your**

What's ...? = What is ...?
What's **your** phone number?
My phone number's 01236 868943.
My phone **number's** = My phone **number is**

Note: You can say **oh** *or* **zero** *for 0 in phone numbers.*

···> **Grammar reference 5 and 8**

---

3 **a** ▶▶ 16 Listen to a telephone conversation and write the numbers.

Richard Banks

Address:
Orange Design, 25 Wood Street
Manchester, MU29 6DL

Telephone: 0161 ....
Mobile phone: ....
Fax: ....

email address: r.cane@orange-design.com

---

b Vocabulary practice ···> Page 94, Exercise 1.

c Say the numbers on the business card in 3a.
The telephone number's ... .
The mobile phone number's ... .
The fax number's ... .

d Grammar practice ···> Page 95, Exercise 2.

4 **a** ▶▶ 17 Listen and match the pairs.

1 r.cane@   a ccs.fr
2 service@   b east.jp
3 k-suzuki@   c cnv.de
4 f_carlton@   d orange-design.com
5 prince_1@   e u-mail.ru
6 smirnov@   f netgate.co.uk

b Practise saying the email addresses in 4a.

5 Communication practice 4. Student A ···> Page 78. Student B ···> Page 88.

6 Talk to other students. Find out their email addresses.

USEFUL LANGUAGE

Numbers 0–10

0	1	2	3	4	5
zero/oh	one	two	three	four	five

6	7	8	9	10
six	seven	eight	nine	ten

Telephone numbers
578956 five seven eight nine five six
44 four four *or* double four
60 six zero *or* six oh
telephone number *or* phone number

email addresses
.   dot
-   dash
_   underscore
@   at

What's your phone / fax / mobile phone number?
What's your email address?

---

1 **a** ▶▶ 18 **Listen and repeat the numbers.**

11 12 13 14 15 16
17 18 19 20 30 40
50 51

b ▶▶ 19 PRONUNCIATION **Listen and repeat.
Practise saying the numbers.**

/iːn/	/i/
13	30
14	40
15	50

c Vocabulary practice ···> Page 95, Exercise 3.

d Work with a partner. Student A says a number (11–59) and Student B writes it. Take it in turns.

2 **a** ▶▶ 20 **Listen to the airport announcements. Fill in the flight times.**

Chicago O'Hare – Terminal 5 Departures

FLIGHT	TO	DEPARTURE	
LH 9150	FRANKFURT MAIN	1	*14:13*
AA 111	ROME	2	
BA 0297	LONDON HEATHROW	3	
MX 3012	MEXICO CITY	4	
IB 7613	MADRID	5	
AA 1955	TORONTO PEARSON	6	

b Work with a partner. Student A says a time, then Student B says the flight. Change roles.

A Fourteen thirteen.
B The flight to Frankfurt.
A That's right.

3 **a** **Match the pairs.**

1	09.00		**a**	seven pm / seven o'clock in the evening
2	12.00		**b**	three pm / three o'clock in the afternoon
3	15.00		**c**	eleven pm / eleven o'clock at night
4	19.00		**d**	nine am / nine o'clock in the morning
5	23.00		**e**	midnight
6	00.00		**f**	midday/noon
7	13.00		**g**	five am / five o'clock in the morning
8	05.00		**h**	one pm / one o'clock in the afternoon

b ▶▶ 21 **Check your answers. Listen and repeat.**

c **Match the times to the clocks. Write a–e in the boxes.**

1 [c] It's quarter past eleven.
2 [ ] It's ten past twelve.
3 [ ] It's five to eight.
4 [ ] It's quarter to five.
5 [ ] It's half past nine.

d ▶▶ **22** **Listen and repeat the questions and the times.**

What time ...?

What time is it?
What's the time? (= What is the time?)

⋯▶ Grammar reference 8

e Vocabulary practice ⋯▶ Page 95, Exercise 4.

4 Communication practice 5 ⋯▶ Page 79. Work with a partner.

5 a ▶▶ **23** **Listen to this conversation at O'Hare Airport station.**

A **Excuse me, what's the time?**
B **It's** quarter past ten.
A **When's the next train?**
B **It's at** ten twenty-three.
A **OK. Thanks.**

b **Practise the conversation in pairs.**

When ...?

When's ...? = When is ...?

⋯▶ Grammar reference 8

c Grammar practice ⋯▶ Page 95, Exercise 5.

TIMETABLE
BLUE LINE
O'Hare Airport – Train Departures

10 am	10:00 10:08 10:15 10:23 10:30 10:38 10:45 10:53
11 am	11:00 11:08 11:15 11:23 11:30 11:38 11:45 11:53
Noon	12:00 12:08 12:15 12:23 12:30 12:38 12:45 12:53
1 pm	1:00 1:08 1:15 1:23 1:30 1:38 1:45 1:53

d **Work with a partner. Look at the timetable for O'Hare Airport station. Practise the conversation from 5a. Use these times.**

1 10.10 2 2.25 3 3.10 4 4.05
5 4.40 6 4.50

USEFUL LANGUAGE

Numbers 11–59

11	12	13	14	15
eleven	twelve	thirteen	fourteen	fifteen

16	17	18	19
sixteen	seventeen	eighteen	nineteen

20	30	40	50	51
twenty	thirty	forty	fifty	fifty-one

Times
What time is it? / What's the time?

What time's the next train? / When's the next train?
It's **at** fourteen thirty.

in the morning/afternoon/evening
at night
at noon/midnight

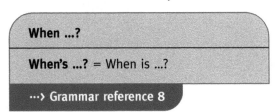

15

2.3 | Buying food

GRAMMAR	Plurals *How much ...?*
VOCABULARY	Numbers 60–100 Prices Food

1 **a** ▶▶ **24** Listen and repeat the numbers.

60 70 80 90 100

b Vocabulary practice ···> Page 95, Exercise 6.

c Work with a partner. Student A says a number (1–100) and student B writes it. Take it in turns.

2 **a** What's the currency in your country? How do you say it in English?

b How much is a Big Mac in your country?

c ▶▶ **25** Listen to the prices. Fill in the gaps in the Big Mac index.

The Economist
Big Mac index

Country	Big Mac price	Big Mac price in dollars
USA	$2.51	$2.51
Brazil	real 2.95	¹$ *1.65*
China	yuan 9.90	$1.20
France	²€ _____	$2.62
Germany	€2.55	$2.37
Italy	€2.32	$2.16
Japan	¥294	³$ _____
Poland	zloty 5.50	$1.28
Spain	€2.25	$2.09
Switzerland	Sfr 5.90	⁴$ _____
UK	⁵£ _____	$3.00

d Work with a partner. Take it in turns to ask questions about the prices of Big Macs. Answer in dollars.

A How much is a Big Mac in Germany?

B It's two dollars thirty seven.

Café Menu

Burger
Hotdog
Chips

Sandwiches

Beef
Salad
Cheese
and Tomato
Egg
Tuna
Chicken

3 **a** Write the food from the menu in the chart.

Vegetable	Meat	Fish	Dairy
tomato			

b ▶▶ **26** PRONUNCIATION Listen and fill in the chart with the words from 3a.

O	Oo	oOo
egg		

4 a ▶▶ **27** **Listen to people buying snacks and drinks. Fill in the gaps.**

1 A Could I have a ¹ _burger_ , please?
   B Anything else?
   A Um ... yes, and a ² _____ , please.
   B That's four euros ³ _____ , please.
   A Four ⁴ _____ .
   B Thanks.

2 A Two ⁵ _____ , please.
   B Two?
   A Yes, please. And two ⁶ _____ . How much is that?
   B Um ... eight ⁷ _____ .
   A OK, eight dollars ⁸ _____ .

3 A Two ⁹ _____ , please. And a ¹⁰ _____ .
   B Anything else?
   A No, thanks.
   B OK. That's ¹¹ _____ pounds ¹² _____ .

Plurals

a sandwich › two sandwich**es**
a coffee › three coffee**s**

···> **Grammar reference 7**

---

b ▶▶ **28** **Listen and repeat these phrases from the conversations.**

How much is that?
Anything else?

c ▶▶ **29** PRONUNCIATION **How do you say the *s* sounds? Listen and repeat. Fill in the chart.**

Singular (a/an)   **Plural** (two, three)

	Singular	Plural	/s/	/z/	/ɪz/
1	hotdog	hotdog**s**	☐	✓	☐
2	burger	burger**s**	☐	☐	☐
3	sandwich	sandwich**es**	☐	☐	☐
4	salad	salad**s**	☐	☐	☐
5	drink	drink**s**	☐	☐	☐
6	coffee	coffee**s**	☐	☐	☐
7	tea	tea**s**	☐	☐	☐
8	orange juice	orange juice**s**	☐	☐	☐

d Grammar practice ···> Page 95, Exercise 7.

e Practise the conversations in 4a in pairs.

5 Communication practice 6 ···> Page 79. Work with a partner.

USEFUL LANGUAGE

Numbers

60	70	80
sixty	seventy	eighty

90	100
ninety	a/one hundred

Currencies

$ = dollar   € = euro
¥ = yen   £ = pound

Buying food

Could I have two coffees and two hotdogs, please?
Anything else?
No, thanks.
How much is that?
Twelve euros sixty, please.

---

3 | Work

1 a Match the words to the photos 1–6.

| factory   hotel   lab   office   warehouse   shop |

1 _hotel_

2 ....

3 ....

4 ....

5 ....

6 ....

b Match the jobs to the workplaces in the chart. Some jobs match to more than one workplace.

| accountant   personal assistant   engineer   manager   receptionist
sales assistant   technician   designer |

Factory	Hotel	Lab	Office	Warehouse	Shop
	receptionist		receptionist		

c ▶▶ 30 Listen and repeat the jobs in 1b.

d Vocabulary practice ···> Page 95, Exercise 1.

18

e ▶▶ 31 **Listen to two people talking about their jobs. Fill in the chart.**

	Person 1	Person 2
Company	Santia Partners	Irex Chemicals
Job		
Workplace		

f **Complete the sentences so they are true for you. Then practise saying them.**

1 I work for _____ .
2 I'm a/an _____ .
3 I work in a/an _____ .
4 I live in _____ .

2 a **Match the questions and answers from the conversation in 1e. Write a–d in the boxes.**

1 [b] What do you do?
2 [ ] What company do you work for?
3 [ ] Where do you work?
4 [ ] Do you live in Boston?

a Irex Chemicals.
b I'm an accountant.
c Yes.
d In a factory in Boston.

b ▶▶ 31 **Listen again and check your answers.**

c ▶▶ 32 **PRONUNCIATION How do you say *do you* in these questions? Listen and repeat. Then practise saying the questions in 2a.**

1 What do you do?
   /djə/
2 Where do you work?
   /djə/

Present simple

Positive
I **live** in London.
I **work** for BDA.

Questions
Where **do** you **work**?
Do you **live** in Paris?

···> **Grammar reference 9**

d Grammar practice ···> Page 95, Exercise 2.

3 Communication practice 7. Student A ···> Page 79. Student B ···> Page 88.

4 **Talk to other students. Ask them about their job and company.**

USEFUL LANGUAGE

What do you do?
I'm a manager/receptionist/technician.
I'm an accountant/assistant/engineer.

What company do you work for?
I work for Wilson Partners.

Where do you work?
I work in Bilbao, in Spain.
I work in a factory/hotel/lab/shop.
Where do you live?
I live in Tokyo.

3.2 | Describing a company

| GRAMMAR | Present simple: positive and questions (*he/she/it/we/they*) |
| VOCABULARY | High numbers, decimals   Business verbs and nouns |

1 a Read the article about Goran Tatić. Are these sentences true (T) or false (F)?

1 Goran Tatić comes from Germany.   `F`
2 He owns all of the Orion Group.   ☐
3 He has 50,000 employees.   ☐
4 Orion companies buy steel from suppliers in Western Europe.   ☐
5 They sell steel to customers in Western Europe.   ☐
6 They make steel all over the world.   ☐

b Vocabulary practice ⋯⋗ Page 96, Exercise 3.

2 a Read the article about Goran Tatić again. Then fill in the gaps with the correct numbers.

> one   two   three   five   six   thirty   fifty
> hundred   thousand   million   billion   point

1 Goran Tatić is ____thirty____ - _____ years old.

2 Total sales are _____ _____ dollars a year.

3 Orion companies have _____ _____ people.

4 Orion companies sell _____ _____ _____ _____ tonnes of steel a year.

5 Goran Tatić and James Bernard own _____ _____ percent of Orion.

b ⏵⏵ **33** Listen and check your answers.

c Vocabulary practice ⋯⋗ Page 96, Exercise 4.

d ⏵⏵ **34** Listen and repeat. Practise saying the numbers with a partner.

400   850   65,000   270,000   3.2 million
6.8 billion

BUSINESS PEOPLE

Goran Tatić

Multi millionaire Goran Tatić is just 36 years old. He comes from Split in Croatia, but today he lives in Victoria, Australia and has Australian nationality. Mr Tatić owns half of the Orion Group. (His colleague, James Bernard, owns the other 50%). Orion companies have total sales of about $3 billion a year, and about 50,000 people work for the group.

Orion Group companies buy steel from suppliers in Russia, Eastern Europe and Korea and sell it all over the world. They buy and sell 2.5 million tonnes a year. They also make steel in a number of factories in Russia.

3 a ▶▶ **35** Listen and repeat the sentences in the grammar box.

> *Present simple: positive*
>
> They **own** the company.
> He **owns** fifty percent of the company.
> *The verb* have *is irregular:*
> They **have** factories in Russia.
> He **has** Australian nationality.
>
> ···> **Grammar reference 9**

b Grammar practice ···> Page 96, Exercise 5.

c ▶▶ **36** PRONUNCIATION Listen and repeat the verbs. Then fill in the chart.

> lives works has buys sells
> makes owns

/z/	*lives*			
/s/	*works*			

4 a ▶▶ **37** Jane Ross, from Centro Pumps UK, is visiting MetaLin, a supplier in Hamburg. Listen to her conversation with Frank Arzt, MetaLin's factory manager. Are these sentences true (T) or false (F)?

1 MetaLin buys steel from a supplier. ☐
2 MetaLin has a factory in China. ☐
3 MetaLin has customers in a number of countries. ☐

b ▶▶ **37** Listen again. Write the numbers you hear.
1 .... tonnes of steel
2 .... products
3 ....% of sales are in Germany

c ▶▶ **37** Listen again. Underline the correct words in the questions from the conversation.
1 Where *do/does* your steel *come/comes* from?
2 Where *do/does* we *buy/buys* it?
3 *Do/Does* it *come/comes* from Germany?
4 Where *do/does* you *sell/sells* your products?

d ▶▶ **38** PRONUNCIATION Listen and repeat the questions in 4c. How do we say *do* and *does*?

> *Present simple: questions*
>
> What **do** you **sell**?
> **Do** they **have** customers in China?
> Where **does** she **come** from?
> **Does** he **own** the company?
>
> ···> **Grammar reference 9**

e Grammar practice ···> Page 96, Exercise 6.

5 Work with a partner. Ask and answer questions about Goran Tatić.

Where ... come from?   Where ... live?
What company ... own?

6 Communication practice 8. Student A ···> Page 79. Student B ···> Page 88.

> USEFUL LANGUAGE
>
> My colleague comes from Germany.
> They buy steel from suppliers in Russia.
> They have factories in China.
> We sell this product all over the world.
> He owns the company.
> They make computer software.
>
> *High numbers and decimals*
> 250 = two hundred and fifty
> 12, 000 = twelve thousand
> 50,000 = fifty thousand
> 2.5 million = two point five million
> 3 billion = three billion

21

3.3	Talking about daily routines	GRAMMAR	Present simple: negative *be*: negative
		VOCABULARY	Daily routine verbs *before/after*, *early/late*

1   **a**   ▶▶ **39**   Listen. Match a–g to the photos.

> a have lunch   b have dinner
> c have breakfast   d have a break
> e finish work   f start work   g get up

1

6.15 am

2

7.30 am

3

9.00 am

4

12.30 pm

5

3.00 pm

6

5.30 pm

7

7.30 pm

b   Work with a partner. Talk about the people in the photos.

A   What time does he/she get up? When does he/she have breakfast?

B   He/She gets up / has breakfast at …

c   Vocabulary practice ···> Page 96, Exercise 7.

d   Work with a partner. Talk about your daily routine.

A   What time / When do you get up?

B   I get up at 7.30.

A   What time …?

2   **a**   ▶▶ **40**   Listen to this conversation about daily routines. Are these sentences true (T) or false (F)?

1   It's 8.10 am.   [F]

2   The man is five minutes late.   ☐

3   The man has a coffee.   ☐

4   The man starts work at 10.00 am.   ☐

5   The boss finishes at 4.00 pm.   ☐

b   ▶▶ **40**   Listen again. Fill in the gaps in these polite phrases.

1   Good _____ .

2   Sorry I'm _____ .

3   _____ problem.

c Look at these sentences from the conversation. Fill in the gaps with negatives.

doesn't don't isn't aren't not isn't

1 It ___isn't___ late.
2 I'm .... a morning person.
3 We .... work late.
4 We .... evening people.
5 My boss .... a morning person.
6 He .... have lunch.

d ▷▷ 41 Listen and check your answers. Practise saying the sentences in 2d.

e ▷▷ 42 PRONUNCIATION Listen to the words. Do they have one syllable (O) or two (OO)?

		O	OO
1	not	☑	☐
2	aren't	☐	☐
3	isn't	☐	☐
4	doesn't	☐	☐
5	don't	☐	☐

Present simple: negative

be
I'm not a morning person.
You **aren't** late.
He **isn't** late.

Other verbs
They **don't work** late.
She **doesn't start** early.

···> Grammar reference 1 and 9

---

f Grammar practice ···> Page 96, Exercise 8.

3 Communication practice 9 ···> Page 79. Work with a partner.

4 **a** Work with a partner. Read the article about mealtimes. Which two statements are not true?

Greenwich Mealtime?

It's noon Greenwich Meantime: 12.00 in the UK, 7.00 am on the US east coast and 5.30 pm in India. But is it lunchtime in London, breakfast time in Boston and dinner time in Delhi? Mealtimes around the world are as different as Japanese sushi and Swiss cheese.

1 People in Spain have dinner late. They eat at about nine o'clock or ten o'clock in the evening.

2 People in the UK have a big breakfast, with bacon and eggs, and then they don't eat lunch.

3 Workers in France have a long lunch break. They have between one and two hours to eat.

4 In the USA, a lot of people just have half an hour for lunch, and eat a sandwich in the office.

5 In Switzerland, people start work at 7.00 am and have breakfast in the office.

6 And in Japan, a lot of managers have dinner in the evening, and then go back to the office.

b ▷▷ 43 Now listen to six people talking about mealtimes and routines in their countries. Check your answers to 4a.

5 Talk about routines in your country and any other countries you know well.
What time do people start work? Do they start early?
What time do they have lunch?
Do they have coffee breaks?
What time do they finish work? Do people work late?
What time do people have dinner?

USEFUL LANGUAGE

What time do you start/finish work?
What time do you have breakfast/lunch/dinner?

I get up early. I start work at 7.45.
I don't work late. I finish at 5.00.
We don't have coffee breaks.

Jan starts work at 2.00 pm. She starts **after** lunch.
Alan finishes work at 10.30 am. He finishes **before** lunch.

---

4 | Information

1 **a** ▶▶ 44 **Neil Leeman phones Tina Carey, a colleague. Listen to the conversation and answer the questions.**

1 What's Neil's problem?
2 Where can Neil find the answer?

b ▶▶ 44 **Listen again. Fill in the gaps in the sentences.**

> know   mean   spell   stand for   think
> understand

1 I don't __understand__ an abbreviation on page six.
2 It's sales jargon. What does it _____ ?
3 Good question. I don't _____ .
4 Does B _____ 'business'?
5 I'm not sure, but I _____ it's netlingo dot com.
6 How do you _____ 'netlingo'?

c Vocabulary practice ···> Page 96, Exercise 1.

2 **a** **Read the article. What is NetLingo?**

@ email www .com
DVD CD SMS B2B
.biz .co.uk .org

What does the 'e' stand for in 'email'? What does 'com' mean? What does 'www' stand for? If you don't understand the language of the Internet and e-business, the answers are at netlingo.com.

The NetLingo website has an online dictionary with thousands of words, from @ to Zip.

b **Work with a partner. Ask and answer questions about the words and abbreviations at the top of the article.**

A What does ... mean?
B (I think) ... means ... (but I'm not sure).
A What does ... stand for?
B I don't know. / It stands for ... .

3 **a** ▶▶ **45** **Listen to Neil Leeman speaking to a customer on the telephone. Complete the form.**

☎ *Customer*

Name: Linda _____

Company: _____ *Insurance*

---

b ▶▶ **45** **Listen again and complete the conversation. What questions does Neil ask to get the customer information right?**

Customer	My name's Linda Sammerson. And I'm from Hughes Insurance.
Neil	Sorry? ¹ _____ _____ ?
Customer	Linda Sammerson. S-A double M-E-R-S-O-N.
Neil	² _____ _____ ?
Customer	Sorry. S-A double M-E-R-S-O-N.
Neil	S-A double M-E-R-S-O-N.
Customer	That's right. And I'm from Hughes Insurance.
Neil	Hughes? ³ _____ _____ ?
Customer	H-U-G-H-E-S.
Neil	H-U-G-H-E-S.
Customer	That's right.
Neil	OK. Well, thanks very much for your call. I'll check ...

c ▶▶ **46** **Listen and repeat the questions from the conversation.**

Polite requests: **Could ...?**

Could you spell that, please?

⋯⟩ **Grammar reference 15**

d Grammar practice ⋯⟩ Page 97, Exercise 2.

4 Communication practice 10. Student A ⋯⟩ Page 80. Student B ⋯⟩ Page 88.

5 **a** **Does your language use English words? Write some words in the chart.**

Computer/Internet words	Business words

b **Discuss your words with a partner. How do you say them in your language? How do you say them in English?**

USEFUL LANGUAGE

What does 'web' mean?
It means 'Internet'.
What does 'e' stand for?
It stands for 'electronic'.
How do you spell 'Internet'?

I don't understand. What does this mean?
I don't know. / I'm not sure. / I think it means ... .

Sorry? Could you say that again?
Could you speak slowly, please?

---

1 **a** **47 Listen to the people talking about email at work. Fill in the gaps.**

> read   receive   send   write

1 I _send_ ten to fifteen emails a day, to colleagues and friends.
2 I _____ about thirty or forty messages a day, from colleagues and customers.
3 I don't _____ messages in English.
4 I _____ emails in English. I understand about 50%.

b **Work with a partner. Talk about emails in your job, using the verbs in 1a.**

2 **a** **Work in pairs. Read the emails. Who would like to go to the training course and what are their telephone numbers?**

b Vocabulary practice ···> Page 97, Exercise 3.

c **Read the emails and <u>underline</u> all the possessive adjectives from the box.**

> my   your   his   her   its   our   their

a

Delete Reply Forward Print

To: all managers and assistants
From: Susanne Flore – Training Manager – CC Software International (Geneva)
Subject: English training course

Do you send and receive emails in English?
Do you read and write reports in English?
'Write English' is a training course for CC Software's managers and <u>their</u> assistants. The course is at our head office in Geneva.

b

Delete Reply Forward Print

To: Susanne Flore
From: Mario Toro
Subject: English training course

Dear Ms Flore,

Two people from CC Software Italy would like to go to the 'Write English' training course. They are Silvia Lardi, an assistant at our office in Milan, and Antonio Amato, the manager of the Rome office.

Best regards,

Mario Toro
Human Resources Manager – CC Software Italy
m.toro@cc-s.it
Tel: +39 02449690791, extension 22

c

Delete Reply Forward Print

To: Mario Toro
From: Susanne Flore
Subject: email addresses and extension numbers

Dear Mr Toro,

Thank you for your message. Silvia Lardi and Antonio Amato are welcome on the course. Could you send their email addresses and extension numbers?

Best regards,

Susanne Flore
Training Manager – CC Software International
s.flore@cc-s.ch
Tel: +41 2290887250, extension 165

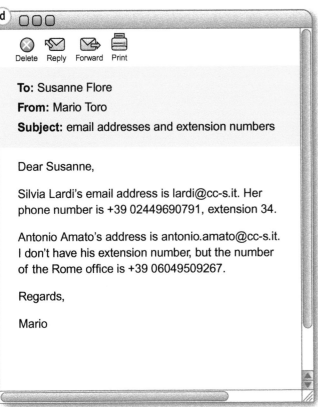

To: Susanne Flore
From: Mario Toro
Subject: email addresses and extension numbers

Dear Susanne,

Silvia Lardi's email address is lardi@cc-s.it. Her phone number is +39 02449690791, extension 34.

Antonio Amato's address is antonio.amato@cc-s.it. I don't have his extension number, but the number of the Rome office is +39 06049509267.

Regards,

Mario

d ▶▶ **48** **Listen and repeat the sentences in the grammar box.**

Possessive adjectives

I work here. This is **my** office.
Where do you work? Where's **your** office?
Tom works here. This is **his** office.
Diana works here. This is **her** office.
The company has **its** office in Berlin.
We work here. This is **our** office.
They work here. This is **their** office.

···**>** Grammar reference 5

Possessive 's and of

Where's Andrew**'s** office?
What's Tom**'s** number?
(*Use* **'s** *with people.*)

He's the manager **of** the Rome office.
What's the number **of** the London office?
(*Use* **of** *with places.*)

···**>** Grammar reference 6

e **Complete 1–5. Use *'s* or *of*. Refer to the emails, if necessary.**

1 +39 02449690791, extension 34
   This is ____*Sylvia's phone number*____ .

2 antonio.amato@cc-s.it
   This is _____ .

3 +39 06049509267
   This is _____ .

4 lardi@cc-s.it
   This is _____ .

5 +41 2290887250, extension 165
   This is _____ .

f Grammar practice ···**>** Page 97, Exercise 4.

3 **Work with a partner. Ask questions about the emails.**
   What's …'s phone number / extension number / email address?

4 Communication practice 11. Student A ···**>** Page 80. Student B ···**>** Page 89.

USEFUL LANGUAGE

to write/send a message to (someone)
to read/receive a message from (someone)
Writing emails or faxes
Dear Mr/Ms Smith,
(John Smith = Mr; Jill Smith = Ms)
Regards, / Best regards,
Could you send … ?

1 **a Talk to a partner:**

Do you read a lot of books? Where do you buy them?

What sort of music do you like? Where do you buy your CDs?

Where do you book your holidays/flights?

b Read about the websites. Do you use these websites?

c Read about the companies again, and fill in the gaps. Use a dictionary to help you.

> computer   copy   download
> files   print   save   software
> book

1 You read e-books on a
   computer .

2 Adobe Reader is ....

3 Customers .... music from itunes.

4 iTunes doesn't sell songs on CDs. The songs are computer
   ....

5 If you download a file, you .... it on your computer's hard drive.

6 iTunes customers .... music from their computers to CDs.

7 iTunes sells CD covers to download and .... on paper.

8 You can .... easyJet flights by phone or online.

d ▶▶ 49 Listen and check your answers.

e Vocabulary practice ⋯▸ Page 97, Exercise 5.

☐☐☐
◀▶ ↻ www.guide-to-topwebsites.com/summary/faq/html

Top websites...

amazon.co.uk

Amazon sells books and hundreds of other products. You pay by credit card and Amazon sends your products by mail. You can also download 'e-books' to read on your computer (with Adobe Reader software).

Q: I can't read e-books – I don't have Adobe Reader. How much is it? Where can I buy it?

A: Adobe Reader is free. You can download the software from the Amazon or Adobe websites.

 iTunes.com

At iTunes you can download music. The site has 700,000 songs. You can save the music on your computer, or copy the files to a CD. And customers can download and print CD covers.

Q: Can I make two or three copies of CDs?

A: If the CDs are for you, yes. But you can't give or sell copies to other people.

easyJet.com
Come on, let's fly!

You can book an easyJet flight at easyjet.com. You pay by credit card. You can also book by phone, but if you do it on the Internet you save €14.

Q: Do I receive my plane tickets by mail?

A: No. easyJet doesn't have tickets. You just get a reference number.

2 **a** Read the text again. <u>Underline</u> the correct words in the sentences.

1 You *can*/*can't* buy books from Amazon.
2 You *can*/*can't* read e-books with Adobe software.
3 You *pay*/*don't pay* for Adobe Reader.
4 You *can*/*can't* buy songs from itunes.
5 You *can*/*can't* buy CDs from iTunes.
6 easyJet flights *are*/*aren't* free on the Internet.
7 easyJet *prints*/*doesn't print* tickets.

---

can

Positive
You **can** buy books from Amazon.
Customers **can** download music from iTunes.

Negative
He **can't** read the file.
You **can't** copy CDs.

Questions
Can you buy products from the website?
What **can** customers buy?
Where **can** I buy CDs?

···> **Grammar reference 14**

---

b Grammar practice ···> Page 97, Exercise 6.

3 **a** ▶▶ 50 Listen to this conversation about booking train tickets online. What's the website address?

b ▶▶ 50 Listen again and answer the questions.

1 What's the name of the train company?
2 What country is the company in?
3 Can you read the website in English?
4 Can you pay for tickets by credit card?
5 Can you receive tickets by mail in the UK?

c ▶▶ 51 **PRONUNCIATION** Listen and repeat these phrases from the conversation. How do you say *can* and *can't* in the sentences?

1 You can book on the Internet.
/kən/

2 And can you pay by credit card?
/kənjuː/

3 You can't receive tickets ... .
/kɑːnt/

4 Communication practice 12. Student A ···> Page 80. Student B ···> Page 89.

5 Think about a website you know. Make notes about what you can use it for. Talk to your partner about it. Ask your partner questions about a website they use.

USEFUL LANGUAGE

 I can open the **file**, but I can't read it.

 This computer has French and German **software**.

 You can **save** photos on the computer.

 You can **print** documents and photos on paper.

 I **copy** all files onto a CD.

 You can **download** the software from the Internet.

---

5 | Places

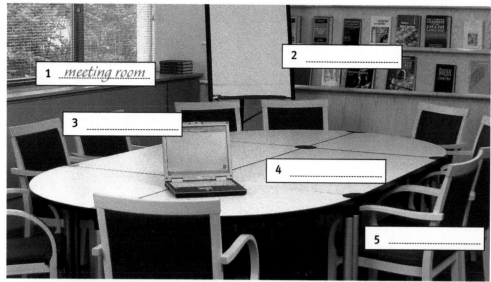

1 *meeting room*
2 _____
3 _____
4 _____
5 _____

8 _____

9 _____

10 _____

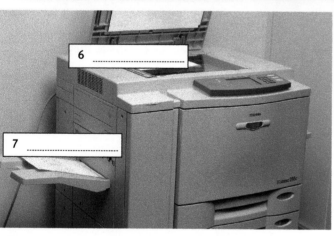

11 _____

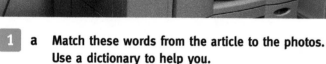

6 _____
7 _____

1 **a** **Match these words from the article to the photos. Use a dictionary to help you.**

> chair   fax machine   laptop   meeting room
> phone   photocopier   photocopy
> power socket   printer   table   flip chart

b ▶▶ **52** **Check your answers. Listen and repeat.**

c **Read the article and answer the questions.**

1 What are 'business facilities'? Give examples.
2 Where is the Emirates Towers Hotel?
3 What group is the hotel in?
4 What is the group's business strategy?
5 Does the hotel have good business facilities?

The Emirates Towers Hotel means business

'Is there a meeting room at the hotel? Are there tables and chairs? We need a photocopy of this – is there a photocopier? Can we use the fax machine? I need to make a phone call. Are there power sockets and Internet connections for laptops? Is there a printer we can use?' There are a thousand questions about business facilities at hotels. At the Emirates Towers Hotel in Dubai, there's just one answer: 'Yes'.
The Emirates Towers is in the Jumeirah International group, where 'Yes' isn't just a word, it's a business strategy ('We don't say "No" to our customers.'). What business facilities are there at the Emirates Towers? The answer is, the hotel doesn't just have business facilities – it *is* a business facility.

d Vocabulary practice ···> Page 97, Exercise 1.

2 a ▶▶ 53 Listen to the conversation between a customer and a receptionist at the Horizon Hotel. Can the man send and receive emails at the hotel?

b ▶▶ 53 Listen again. What facilities are there in the hotel business centre? Tick (✓) the boxes.

1 meeting rooms [✓]
2 photocopier [ ]
3 fax machine [ ]
4 drinks machine [ ]
5 phones [ ]
6 computers [ ]
7 power sockets [ ]

c ▶▶ 54 PRONUNCIATION Listen and repeat.

1 There are meeting rooms.
/ðeə ə/
2 There's a photocopier.
/ðeəz/
3 Are there power sockets?
/ɑːr ðeə/
4 Is there a phone socket?
/ɪz ðeə/

---

there is/are

Singular: **There's** a photocopier in my office. (There's = There is)

Plural: **There are** two printers in the office.

Questions: **Is there** a fax machine here? **Are there** computers at the hotel?

Negative: **There aren't** phones in the meeting rooms. **There isn't** a laptop.

···> Grammar reference 10

---

d Grammar practice ···> Page 98, Exercise 2.

3 a Make verbs from the <u>underlined</u> nouns and fill in the gaps in A's sentences. Use a dictionary to help you.

1 A I need to *photocopy* this. Could I use the <u>photocopier</u>?
   B Yes, ...
2 A I need to .... my assistant. Can I make a <u>phone</u> call from here?
   B Yes, ...
3 A I need to .... this to my office. Could I use the <u>fax machine</u>?
   B Yes, ...
4 A I need to .... this file. Can I send <u>emails</u> from this computer?
   B Yes, ...
5 A I need to .... a copy of this file. Is there a <u>printer</u> I can use?
   B Yes, ...

b ▶▶ 55 Now listen and fill in B's replies.

c Practise the conversations in 3a.

---

need (to)

(need + to + *verb*)
I **need to** photocopy this.

(need + *noun*)
I **need** a copy of this.

···> Grammar reference 16

---

d Grammar practice ···> Page 98, Exercise 3.

4 Communication practice 13. Student A ···> Page 80. Student B ···> Page 89.

USEFUL LANGUAGE

I need to make a phone call. Can I use the phone in the meeting room?

Is there a power socket for my laptop?

I need to print this page. Do you have a printer?

I need to photocopy this. Is there a photocopier here?

You can fax it. We have a fax machine.

Facts & Figures

Petronas Towers – Headquarters of the Petronas oil company in Kuala Lumpur, Malaysia

The senior management offices are on level 86 of the building.

There are ¹ ___2___ entrances/exits: one on the ground floor, one on the first floor.

There are 88 floors in the building above ground level. The basement has four levels.

There is a 'sky bridge' (a corridor in the air) at levels 41 and 42.

The building has ² _____ doors.

There are ³ _____ windows in the building.

There are ⁴ _____ flights of stairs.

The building has ⁵ _____ lifts.

1 **a** **Work with a partner. Can you complete the Facts & Figures about the Petronas Towers with these numbers?**

| 2   76   765   1,800   32,000 |

b ▶▶ **56** **Listen and check your answers.**

2 **a** **Match the words to the buttons in the lift.**

| basement   fifth   first   fourth
| ground   second   sixth   third |

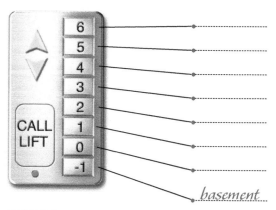

basement

b ▶▶ **57** **Check your answers. Listen and repeat.**

c **Look at the Facts & Figures again. Fill in the gaps in these sentences.**

The entrances to the Petronas Towers are on the ¹ _ground_ and ² _____ floors.

A 'sky bridge' links the two towers on the forty-³ _____ and forty-⁴ _____ floors.

Petronas's senior managers have their offices on the eighty-⁵ _____ floor.

Ordinal numbers

1st = first	5th = fifth	9th = ninth
2nd = second	6th = sixth	10th = tenth
3rd = third	7th = seventh	11th = eleventh
4th = fourth	8th = eighth	12th = twelfth ...

d Vocabulary practice ···> Page 98, Exercise 4.

e **Talk about your office.**

The office building has ... floors. Our office is on the ... floor.

The entrance is on the ... floor.
There's a / There are ... lift(s).

3 **a** **Match the words to the signs.**

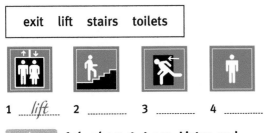

exit   lift   stairs   toilets

1 *lift*   2 ....   3 ....   4 ....

b ▶▶ **58** **Ask where 1–4 are. Listen and repeat the questions.**

c ▶▶ **59** **Listen to the people asking for directions. What are they looking for?**

1 *exit*   3 ....
2 ....   4 ....

d **Look at the office plan. Can you match the questions and answers? Write a–e in the boxes.**

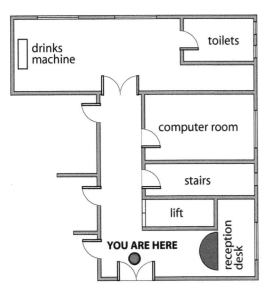

drinks machine

toilets

computer room

stairs

lift

YOU ARE HERE

reception desk

1 Excuse me. Where's the lift? [b]

2 Excuse me. Where are the stairs? ☐

3 Where's the computer room? ☐

4 Where's the drinks machine? ☐

5 Where are the toilets, please? ☐

a On the right, just after the lift.

b It's over there. The first door on the right.

c It's just past the stairs. The third door on the right.

d Go through the doors at the end, and they're on the right.

e Go to the end of the corridor, through the doors, and turn left.

e ▶▶ **60** **Listen and check your answers.**

f Vocabulary practice ···> Page 98, Exercise 5.

g ▶▶ **61** **Listen and repeat the directions.**

1 They're **on the right**.

2 It's **just past** the stairs.

3 Go **through** the doors.

4 Go to **the end of** the corridor.

h **Work with a partner. Take it in turns to ask and answer the questions in 3d.**

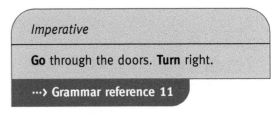

Imperative

Go through the doors. **Turn** right.

···> Grammar reference 11

i Grammar practice ···> Page 98, Exercise 6.

4 Communication practice 14. Student A ···> Page 81. Student B ···> Page 89.

USEFUL LANGUAGE

Excuse me. Where's ...?
It's on the ground/first/second ... floor.
It's over there.
It's just past the lift, on the right.
Go to the end of the corridor.
Go through the doors.
Turn right/left.

5.3 Talking about your home

GRAMMAR Adjectives *quite/very*

VOCABULARY In and around the home

1 a Where are the properties in the two adverts?

1 _house_ 2 _____ 3 _____

4 _____ 5 _____ 6 _____

7 _____

Property

a

12 apartments, central Sydney. Studio, 1, 2 and 3 bedrooms. Top two floors (24th and 25th) of new block.

Prices from $480,000.

b

Gold Coast near Brisbane

(summer 30°C, winter 20°C). 19th century house. 6 bedrooms, 2 bathrooms (upstairs and downstairs), large living room (65 m²), modern kitchen, garage. Garden 3,100 m² with swimming pool. Beautiful view of Tasman Sea.

$1.6 million.

b Find words in the adverts to match the photos 1–8. Use a dictionary to help you.

c ▶▶ 62 Check your answers. Listen and repeat.

d Vocabulary practice ⋯▸ Page 98, Exercise 7.

2 a Read the adverts again. <u>Underline</u> the correct adjectives in 1–8.

1 The apartment block is *modern/old*.
2 The apartments are in a *low/high* building.
3 The house is *old/new*.
4 The living room in the house is *big/small*.
5 The kitchen in the house is *old/new*.
6 There's a *nice/horrible* view from the garden of the house.
7 It's *hot/cold* in Brisbane.
8 The house is *cheap/expensive*.

b Find adjectives in the adverts with a similar meaning.

1 new _modern_
2 big _____
3 nice _____

Adjectives

The apartment **is big**.
It's **a big** apartment.
The rooms in the house **are small**.
The house has **small** rooms.

⋯▸ Grammar reference 12

c Vocabulary practice ⋯▸ Page 98, Exercise 8.

3 **a** Look at the title of the article. What does 'hot property' mean?

b Read the article and answer the questions.

1 How many people live in Australia?

2 Where do most people live?

3 Where is property quite expensive?

4 Where are property prices very low?

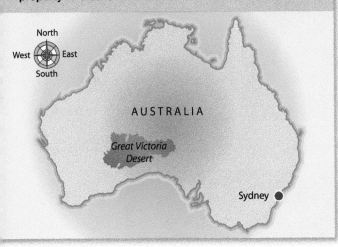

Hot Property in Australia

It has 36,000 km of coast. There are 7.6 million km² of land. Australia is big. Very big. But the population of 18 million is very small for a continent.

With just two people per square kilometre, does this mean Australian property is cheap? Not exactly. A large percentage of Australians live in a small number of big cities on the south-east coast. The large population there means homes are quite expensive (the really hot property is in Sydney).

In parts of Western Australia, the opposite is true. A very small population means very low property prices. For the price of a square metre in Sydney you can buy a square kilometre near the Great Victoria Desert. Hot property of a different kind!

c Now discuss these questions with a partner.

1 What do 'm' and 'km' stand for?

2 What does the writer mean by 'hot property of a different kind'?

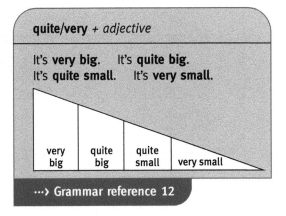

quite/very + *adjective*

It's **very big**. It's **quite big**.
It's **quite small**. It's **very small**.

| very big | quite big | quite small | very small |

···> Grammar reference 12

4 **a** ▶▶| **63** Listen to a man talking to a colleague about his home. <u>Underline</u> the correct words.

1 The house is *quite/very small/big*.

2 The garden is *quite/very small/big*.

3 The house is *quite/very old/modern*.

4 Property is *quite/very cheap/expensive*.

b Grammar practice ···> Page 99 Exercise 9.

5 Communication practice 15. Student A ···> Page 81. Student B ···> Page 90.

6 **a** Work with a partner. Talk about each other's homes.

Where ... live?   ... house/apartment?   ... big? ... garage/garden?

b Talk about property prices in your country.

Are property prices high?

In what cities/regions is property expensive/cheap?

In what parts of your town/region is property expensive/cheap?

USEFUL LANGUAGE

I live in a house / an apartment in ... .

It's ... kilometres from .... .

The house/apartment is quite/very big/large/small. It's ... square metres.

It's old/modern. It's quite/very nice.

It has ... bedrooms. It has a big/small garden.

Is property expensive in your country?

In ... prices are quite/very high, but in ... .

6 | Action

1 **a** Label the photos (a–e) with the words in the box.

> go on business trips   go to conferences
> have meetings   give presentations
> go to trade fairs

b Discuss these questions with a partner.

Do you go to conferences?

Do you have a lot of meetings?

Do you give presentations?

Do you go on business trips?

Do you go to trade fairs?

c ▶▶ **64** Listen to five people talking about their jobs. Match the people you hear to the photos. Write 1–5 in the boxes.

d Vocabulary practice ···> Page 99, Exercise 1.

> *Adverbs of frequency*
>
> He **often** goes to the head office.
> They're **always** late for meetings.
>
> ←——— always usually often sometimes don't often never
> 100%   0%
>
> ···> Grammar reference 17

a

_____

b

_____

c *1*

have meetings

d

_____

e

_____

2 **a** Look at the adverbs of frequency in the grammar box. Then complete the sentences so they are true for you.

1 I _____ give presentations.

2 I _____ go on business trips.

3 I _____ work in the evening.

4 I _____ write emails in English.

5 I _____ work at home.

b ▶▶ **65** Listen to an interview with Veronica Stephens, a television producer. How often does she do these things? Tick (✓) the boxes.

		always	usually	often	sometimes	never
1	works for television companies in Japan	☐	✓	☐	☐	☐
2	works with presenters from Japan	☐	☐	☐	☐	☐
3	makes programmes in English	☐	☐	☐	☐	☐
4	works with a team from Japan	☐	☐	☐	☐	☐
5	works with a team from the UK	☐	☐	☐	☐	☐
6	goes to Japan on business	☐	☐	☐	☐	☐

c Work with a partner. Make sentences about Veronica.

She usually works with television companies in Japan.

3 **a** ▶▶ **66** Listen to Stuart Compton talking to a colleague about work. Are the sentences true (T) or false (F)?

1 He doesn't have a lot of meetings. ☐ T

2 He travels a lot on business. ☐

3 He doesn't make a lot of phone calls. ☐

4 He sends a lot of emails. ☐

a lot (of) / lots (of)

a lot of/lots of + *noun*
We have **a lot of** customers in France.
We have **lots of** customers in Italy too.
(a lot of / lots of = a large number)

verb + **a lot**
I go abroad **a lot.** (= often)

···▶ **Grammar reference 17**

b ▶▶ **67** PRONUNCIATION Listen and repeat. How do you say *of* in the sentences?

1 I have a lot of meetings.

2 I don't give a lot of presentations.

3 Do you go to a lot of conferences?

c Grammar practice ···▶ Page 99, Exercise 2.

4 Communication practice 16 ···▶ Page 81. Work with a partner.

USEFUL LANGUAGE

Do you often travel on business?
I don't often go abroad on business trips.
I often send emails to foreign colleagues.
I make a lot of international phone calls.
I sometimes go to trade fairs and conferences.
I never give presentations in English.
I go to a lot of meetings in English.

1 **a** ▶▶ **68** **Listen to the conversation in the meeting. Fill in the gaps.**

| having phoning working moment |
| now moment this today |

Jim Emma, I'm ¹ _having_ a meeting at the ² _____ with Laura and Chris.

Emma Right.

Jim You're on the loud speaker.

Emma OK. Hi everyone.

Laura Hello, Emma.

Chris Are you having a good time in Istanbul?

Emma Oh, it's great. Really good. The only problem is, I'm ³ _____ !

Chris I'm sure you aren't working all the time!

Jim Emma, we're ⁴ _____ about your project. Can we ask you one or two questions?

Emma Sure. Go ahead.

Jim OK. Chris?

Chris Yeah. What's your team doing ⁵ _____ , Emma?

Emma Well, they aren't working at the ⁶ _____ . They're having lunch.

Chris No, I mean on the project. What are they working on ⁷ _____ week?

Emma Oh, right. Um ... Well, ⁸ _____ we're working on installation number six. We're just finishing the testing on that – that's the last job ...

b Vocabulary practice ⋯> Page 99, Exercise 3.

c **What are Jim, Laura, Chris and Emma doing at the moment? Write the correct form of the verb. Refer to the conversation in 1a again, if necessary.**

1 Jim, Laura and Chris are in the office this morning. _They're having_ a meeting. *(have)*

2 Emma isn't in the office this week. _____ on a project in Istanbul. *(work)*

3 Emma's in Istanbul. _____ a good time. *(have)*

4 Emma's at work at the moment. _____ a phone call. *(make)*

5 Emma's colleagues are having lunch. _____ at the moment. *(not work)*

6 Laura's in a meeting. She _____ lunch at the moment. *(not have)*

7 Jim, Chris and Laura are talking. _____ Emma questions. *(ask)*

8 Emma and her colleagues are on the last job. _____ the testing. *(finish)*

Present continuous

Positive
I**'m working** on the report now.
She**'s making** a phone call.
They**'re having** lunch at the moment.

Negative
I**'m not having** a coffee at the moment.
He **isn't making** a phone call.
OR
He**'s not making** a phone call.
We **aren't working** today.
OR
We**'re not** working today.
Both forms of the negative are in common use.

Questions
What's she **doing**? (What's = What is)
What **are** you **doing**?
Is he **having** a meeting?
Are they **working** on the project?

···> Grammar reference 18

2 ▶▶ **70** **Listen to the telephone conversations. What are the people doing? Complete the sentences.**

1 Steve's _____ *having lunch* _____ .
2 Olivia's _____ .
3 Colin's _____ .
4 Nadia's _____ .
5 Paolo's _____ .
6 Sylvia's _____ .

3 Communication practice 17. Student A ···>
Page 81. Student B ···> Page 90.

4 **Talk to a partner. What are you working on at the moment?**

d ▶▶ **69** **PRONUNCIATION Listen and repeat the sentences. How do you say -*ing*?**

1 I'm having a meeting.
2 What's she doing?
3 She isn't working today.
4 We're all working on the project.
5 Are they having lunch now?
6 What are you doing?

e Grammar practice ···> Page 99, Exercise 4.

USEFUL LANGUAGE

He's in a meeting this morning.
They're having a coffee at the moment.
What are you doing now?
I'm not in the office today.
We're working on the new project this week.

6.3 | Saying what you do in your spare time

GRAMMAR	Gerund
VOCABULARY	Sports and leisure activities

1 a Read the text. Can you buy *For Dummies* books in your country?

b Answer the questions.

1 What is 'spare time'?
2 Why do people buy *For Dummies* books?
3 What kind of people buy *For Dummies* books?
4 Is the *For Dummies* series successful?

"This book rates two fins up"
for a nymar wanting a crash course on fishing." Saltwatr Vacation magazine

Fishing
FOR
DUMMIES

Peter Kaminsky
Outdoors Columnist for
The New York Times

A Reference for the Rest of Us!

"I give this book 'two tips up!'"
— Trace Worthington, senior three World Freestyle Skiing Champion and two-time Olympian

Skiing
FOR
DUMMIES

Allen St. John
Contributing editor, Skiing magazine
Foreword by Jonny Moseley
1998 Olympic Gold Medal Winner
Freestyle Skiing

A Reference for the Rest of Us!

What do you do in your spare time?
Not a lot? Are you looking for a new hobby? If you are, then a good place to start is the *For Dummies* books. The books teach you how to do hundreds of things, from American football to Chinese cooking. *For Dummies* books explain all the basics in simple language, so they're perfect for absolute beginners. The black and yellow books now have hundreds of titles in 39 languages. With 100 million copies in print, it's obvious that free time is big business.

c Match the words to the activities in the pictures.

> aerobics   basketball   chess   cycling
> fishing   football   guitar   running   skiing
> swimming   walking   weight training

1 _____guitar_____

2 _____

3 _____

4 _____

5 _____

6 _____

7 _____

8 _____

9 _____

10 _____

11 _____

12 _____

d ▶▶ **71** PRONUNCIATION Check your answers. Listen and repeat. Are any of the words the same or similar in your language? Is their pronunciation different in English?

2 **a** ▶▶ **72** Listen to two colleagues talking about leisure. Which activities from 1c do they talk about?

b ▶▶ **72** Listen again. Complete this extract from the conversation.

A Don't you like ¹_____ ?

B I hate ²_____ .

A Oh, I love ³_____ . It's good for you, as well.

B Not if you can't ⁴_____ !

A No, that's true!

c Fill in the gaps. Then make four sentences that are true for you.

like don't like love hate

 1 I _____love_____ skiing!

 2 I _____ walking.

 3 I _____ swimming.

4 I _____ running!

> *Gerund*
>
> I hate walk**ing**.
> I like ski**ing**.
>
> ···> Grammar reference 19

d Grammar practice ···> Page 99, Exercise 5.

e Look at the photos. Can you guess what the people do in their spare time?

f ▶▶ **73** Now listen to the people and fill in the gaps.

1 I play _____ .
I do _____ .
I go _____ .

2 I play _____ .
I do _____ .
I go _____ .

3 I play _____ .
I play the _____ .
I go _____ .

> **go/play/do**
>
> I **go** + *nouns with* -ing
> I **play** + *sports, games, musical instruments*
> I **do** + aerobics, weight training

g Vocabulary practice ···> Page 99, Exercise 6.

3 Communication practice 18 ···> Page 82. Work with a partner.

> USEFUL LANGUAGE
>
> What do you do in your spare time?
> I go cycling.
> I do aerobics.
> I play football/the guitar.
> I love/like/hate swimming.

41

7 | Meeting

Planner

① ② ③ ④

JANUARY						
M	**T**	**W**	**T**	**F**	**S**	**S**
				1	2	3
4	5	6	7	8	9	10
11	12	13	14	15	16	17
18	19	20	21	22	23	24
25	26	27	28	29	30	31

FEBRUARY						
M	**T**	**W**	**T**	**F**	**S**	**S**
1	2	3	4	5	6	7
8	9	10	11	12	13	14
15	16	17	18	19	20	21
22	23	24	25	26	27	28

MARCH						
M	**T**	**W**	**T**	**F**	**S**	**S**
1	2	3	4	5	6	7
8	9	10	11	12	13	14
15	16	17	18	19	20	21
22	23	24	25	26	27	28
29	30	31				

APRIL						
M	**T**	**W**	**T**	**F**	**S**	**S**
			1	2	3	4
5	6	7	8	9	10	11
12	13	14	15	16	17	18
19	20	21	22	23	24	25
26	27	28	29	30		

1 a ▶▶ 74 Listen to four short conversations. When do the people arrange to meet? Mark the four dates on the calendar.

b ▶▶ 75 Listen and repeat the months.

January February March April May June July August September October November December

c ▶▶ 75 PRONUNCIATION Listen again and fill in the chart.

oOo	O	Ooo	Oo	oO
		January		

Dates

We write:	We say:
May 11th	May the eleventh
11th May	the eleventh of May

d Vocabulary practice ···> Page 100, Exercise 1.

e ▶▶ 76 **Listen. Write the days in the order you hear them.**

| Monday Tuesday Wednesday |
| Thursday Friday Saturday Sunday |

1 _Wednesday_   5 ....

2 ....   6 ....

3 ....   7 ....

4 ....

f ▶▶ 77 **Listen and repeat. Practise saying the days of the week.**

g **Work with a partner. Look at the calendar. You say a date and your partner says the day. Change roles.**

A The twelfth of January.

B Tuesday.

2 a ▶▶ 74 **Listen to the conversations in 1a again. Fill in the gaps in the sentences with *at*, *in* or *on*.**

1 I'm free _at_ the end of January.

Yes, I can make it .... the twenty-eighth.

2 I'm free .... February.

I'm busy .... the beginning of February.

3 Are you free .... the middle of March?

No, I can't make it .... Friday.

4 .... the morning?

.... nine o'clock?

Prepositions with times and dates	
on	Tuesday
	July 9th *(dates)*
in	March *(months)*
	summer *(seasons)*
	the middle of ...
	the morning/afternoon/evening
at	ten o'clock *(times)*
	the beginning/end of
	night
	the weekend
	Christmas

···> Grammar reference 13

b Grammar practice ···> Page 100, Exercise 2.

c Vocabulary practice ···> Page 100, Exercise 3.

d **Work with a partner. Student A points to one of the phrases and Student B asks a question. Take it in turns.**

A Friday.

B Are you free on Friday?

- Tuesday
- end of March
- the morning
- six o'clock
- Friday
- two o'clock
- middle of December
- August 10th
- the weekend
- the evening

3 ▶▶ 78 PRONUNCIATION **Listen and repeat. How do you say *-th* at the end of the numbers?**

1 What about the twenty-eigh<u>th</u>?

2 I'm free on the four<u>th</u> of February.

3 Friday the twel<u>fth</u>?

4 Yes, the seventeen<u>th</u> of May is fine.

5 No, I can't make it on Friday the thirteen<u>th</u>.

6 So, Monday the fifteen<u>th</u>.

4 Communication practice 19. Student A ···> Page 82. Student B ···> Page 90.

USEFUL LANGUAGE
When can we meet?
When are you free?
What about the tenth of June?
That's fine.
No, I'm busy on the tenth.
I can/can't make it at the end of June.
I'm free at the beginning of July.
I'm busy in the middle of July.
What about the first week in August?

1 **a** ▶▶ **79** **Listen to Gary Lipton talking to a colleague about his plans for a business trip. Fill in the gaps in his diary.**

> Paris   London   Chicago   London

May

Monday 10
Flight: LA 9.00 am →
Arrive New York 5.25 pm
New York 6.15 pm →

Tuesday 11
→ Arrive ¹_____ 6.25 am
Meeting – Tanya Dolan, 9.00 am

Wednesday 12
Meeting – Sue Redman, 9.00 am
Meeting – James Barker, 1.30 pm
Train (Eurostar) to ²_____ (pm)
Hotel Citadelle

Thursday 13
Paris

Friday 14
Paris

Saturday 15
Return to ³_____ (am)
Flight: London 4.35 pm →
⁴_____ 7.00 pm Chicago
10.15 pm →

Sunday 16
→ LA 12.25 am

b **Read Gary's diary again and answer the questions.**

1 Is Gary leaving LA on Tuesday?
2 Where's he changing flights on the way to London?
3 Is he taking the train to Paris on Wednesday?
4 In Paris, which hotel is he staying at?
5 Is he coming back to London on Saturday?
6 Is he arriving in Chicago in the morning?

c **In the sentences Gary Lipton describes his travel plans. Fill in the gaps.**

> take   arrive   change   come back
> leave   stay

1 I *'m leaving* Los Angeles on Monday.
2 I _____ the train – the Eurostar.
3 Then I _____ in Paris for three nights.
4 I _____ back to London on the train.
5 I _____ in LA in the middle of the night.
6 Then, on the flight home, I _____ in Chicago.

Present continuous: future arrangements

I'm flying to London on Monday.
She's meeting a colleague this afternoon.
They're arriving tomorrow.
We're having a meeting at four o'clock.

···> Grammar reference 20

d ▶▶ 79 Listen again and check your answers.

e Vocabulary practice ···> Page 100, Exercise 4.

f Grammar practice ···> Page 100, Exercise 5.

g Can you complete these questions from Gary's conversation in 1a?

| How   When   Where   Who   Why |

1 _When_ are you going to Europe, Gary? Next week?

2 _____ are you going? To the London office?

3 _____ are you meeting? Tanya Dolan again?

4 _____ are you going to Paris? On business?

5 _____ are you travelling to Paris? Are you driving?

h ▶▶ 79 Look at the transcript on page 121 and listen to Gary's conversation again. Check your answers.

i ▶▶ 80 PRONUNCIATION Listen and repeat. How do you say the underlined words?

1 Who's she meeting?
2 Who are you travelling with?
3 Who's coming to the meeting?
4 Why are you leaving early?
5 Why's he going to London?
6 Why are they staying in that hotel?

Who ...? Why ...?

Who are you working with?
I'm working with John.
Who's going to the meeting?
Anne, Peter and Ken.

Why are you going to Hamburg?
I'm going to a meeting.
Why's he taking the train?
Because he doesn't like flying.

···> Grammar reference 8

2 Work with a partner. Look back at Gary's diary. Ask and answer questions about his trip.

A When's Gary leaving/arriving in ...?
B He's leaving/arriving at ... .
A What's he doing on ...?
B He's flying/meeting/going ... .
A Where's he ...? / Who's he ...? / Why's he ...? / How's he ...?

3 Communication practice 20. Student A ···> Page 82. Student B ···> Page 90.

4 Talk to other students. Find out what arrangements they have for this week.

USEFUL LANGUAGE

Where are you going?
Why are you going to Milan?
When/What time are you leaving?
Who are you meeting?
How are you travelling?
I'm leaving London on Tuesday.
I'm arriving/changing in Paris.
She's staying for a week.
He's flying.
They're taking the train.

7.3 Buying train tickets

GRAMMAR *would like to   want to*

VOCABULARY Train tickets and reservations

1 **a** **Talk to other students about train travel.**

How often do you travel by train?

Do you like train travel?

Do you usually reserve a seat?

b **Gary Lipton is buying a ticket for the Eurostar. Read the conversation. Fill in the gaps.**

Assistant	Hello.
Gary	Hi. I'd like to book two seats to Paris, please. For tomorrow.
Assistant	At ¹ _what_ time?
Gary	At about 5.00 pm. I don't have a timetable.
Assistant	² _____'s a train at 17.15. It ³ _____ in Paris at 20.55, local time.
Gary	Right. OK, ⁴ _____'s fine.
Assistant	Would you like to travel first class or standard class?
Gary	Standard.
Assistant	And would you ⁵ _____ a single or a return ticket?
Gary	A round-trip, please.
Assistant	When would you like to ⁶ _____ back?
Gary	I want to return on Saturday, but I don't know what ⁷ _____ .
Assistant	Do you want to book the return trip now?
Gary	If I reserve a seat, ⁸ _____ I change the reservation?
Assistant	With a standard fare, you can change or cancel the booking, yes.
Gary	OK. How ⁹ _____ is the standard fare, then?
Assistant	One moment.

c ▶▶ **81** **Listen and check your answers.**

d **Fill in 1–9 with words from the conversation in 1a.**

1   a one-way ticket (US) = a _single_ (UK)

2   a round-trip ticket (US) = a _____ (UK)

3   a list of times (of trains) = a _____

4   the time at the destination = _____

5   to come back = to _____

6   to book = to _____

7   a booking = a _____

8   a ticket price = a _____

9   normal (ticket, class) = _____

e ▶▶ **82** **Check your answers. Listen and repeat.**

f Vocabulary practice ⋯▸ Page 100, Exercise 6.

2 **a** ▶▶ 84 **Listen to this customer booking a train ticket. Complete the information (1–8).**

1 Destination   *Birmingham*
2 Ticket *(single/return)*: ....
3 Leaving on *(day)*:   ....
4 Leaving at *(time)*:   ....
5 Returning on *(day)*:   ....
6 Returning at *(time)*:   ....
7 Class: ....
8 Fare: £....................................

b **Work with a partner. Look at the transcript for 2a on page 122 and practise the conversation.**

g ▶▶ 83 PRONUNCIATION **How do you say *to* in these sentences? Listen and repeat.**

1 I'd like to book a seat.
2 When would you like to come back?
3 I want to return on Saturday.
4 Do you want to book the return trip now?

3 Communication practice 21. Student A ···▸ Page 82. Student B ···▸ Page 91.

want to + *infinitive* / **would like to** + *infinitive*

I'd like to book a seat.
I want to book a seat.

When **would you like to** leave?
When **do you want to** leave?

Note: would like to *is more formal/polite than* want to.

···▸ Grammar reference 21

USEFUL LANGUAGE

I'd like a return to (Birmingham), please.
Would you like to book/reserve a seat?
When do you want to leave / come back?
Do you want to travel first class or second/standard/economy class?
How much is the standard fare?
Can I change my booking/reservation?

Tickets
a single ticket (UK) / a one-way ticket (US)
return ticket (UK) / round-trip ticket (US)

h Grammar practice ···▸ Page 101, Exercise 7.

8 Reporting

GRAMMAR *be*: past simple *How many...?*

VOCABULARY Time references to the past

1 **a** ▶▶ **85** **Listen to Hanna Day talking to a colleague about a trade fair she visited in India. <u>Underline</u> the correct words.**

1 The trade fair was *yesterday/<u>last week</u>*.

2 The trade fair was *quite/very* good.

3 There were about *100/400* companies at the trade fair.

4 Hanna was in Calcutta *last year/two years ago*.

5 The trade fair in Calcutta *was/wasn't* very big.

6 Hanna and her colleagues *were/weren't* in the same hotel.

b **Can you complete these questions from 1a? Fill in the gaps.**

how   was   many   were   where

1 ___*Were*___ you at the trade fair last week?

2 _____ was it? Delhi?

3 _____ was it? OK?

4 _____ it big?

5 How _____ companies were there?

c ▶▶ **85** **Listen again and check your answers.**

d ▶▶ **86** **PRONUNCIATION Listen and repeat. How do you say *was(n't)* and *were(n't)* in these sentences?**

1 Were you at the trade fair?
/ʒ/

2 Where was it?
/ɒ/

3 It was big.
/ə/

4 I wasn't there last year.
/ɒ/

5 There were thousands of people.
/ə/

6 We weren't in the same hotel.
/ʒ/

---

be: *past simple*

Positive
The conference **was** good last week.
They **were** in the same hotel.

Questions
How many people **were** there?
Was John there?

Negative
The big companies **weren't** at the trade fair.
The presentation **wasn't** very good.

···▶ **Grammar reference 22**

e Grammar practice ···▶ Page 101, Exercise 1.

f   Work with a partner. Talk about where you were:

- yesterday evening
- last Saturday
- a week ago

Time references to the past

	Tuesday	
	March	
last	week/month/year	
	summer	
	Christmas	
two days		
three months	**ago**	
a year		

g   Vocabulary practice ···> Page 101, Exercise 2.

h   Make sentences. Use the words in brackets and past time expressions.

1   Today is Thursday. *(Monday)*
Monday was three days ago.

2   It's November. *(October)*
_____

3   This year. *(2001)*
_____

4   It's Friday. *(last Friday)*
_____

5   Today is Thursday. *(Wednesday)*
_____

6   This month. *(May)*
_____

3   a   Communication practice 22. Student A ···> Page 83. Student B ···> Page 91.

b   Look again at your information from Communication practice 22. Write an email telling your boss about the conference/ training course you went to. Use the email in Exercise 2 to help you.

To: ...
From: ...
Subject: ...

Dear ...,

USEFUL LANGUAGE

How was the trade fair last week?
It was/wasn't very good.
There were a lot of people there.
There weren't a lot of new products.
Where was it?
Who was there?
Was the meeting long?
How many people were at the meeting?

Time references to the past
yesterday, last Friday, last week, last month, last year, three days ago

2   Read this email from Hanna Day to her manager, Luke Roscoe. Fill in the gaps with the correct form of *be*.

To: Luke Roscoe
From: Hanna Day
Subject: trade fair report

Dear Luke,
I'm now back in Vancouver after my trip to Delhi. The trade fair ¹_____*was*_____ very good. It
²_____ a big event – there ³_____ about 400 companies. There ⁴_____ only
two new products at the show, so there ⁵_____ a lot of big sales presentations. But there
⁶_____ a very good presentation, by Mercury Consulting, on new technology. I'm writing
a report about it at the moment. I can send you a copy later this week.
How ⁷_____ business last week? ⁸_____ you busy?
Regards,
Hanna
PS: Edwin Palmer ⁹_____ at the trade show. ¹⁰_____ he in the office?

c ▶▶ 87 **Listen again. <u>Underline</u> the correct words in these sentences about Martin.**

1 He <u>presented</u> / didn't present the business plan.
2 He talked about / didn't talk about the cost of materials.
3 He discussed / didn't discuss suppliers with Miguel.
4 He visited / didn't visit the factory.
5 He looked at / didn't look at the new production line.

1 a ▶▶ 87 **Listen to Martin Berg giving an update to his manager, Hanna Day, about his business trip last week. Was it a good trip?**

b ▶▶ 87 **Listen again. Are these sentences true (T) or false (F)?**

1 Martin travelled to Mexico on Thursday. `F`
2 He worked all day on Friday. ☐
3 He stayed in a hotel near the office. ☐
4 Martin's presentation started at 9.00. ☐
5 The presentation finished at 9.30. ☐
6 This morning, Miguel phoned Martin. ☐

d ▶▶ 88 **Listen and check your answers. Practise saying the sentences.**

e Vocabulary practice ···> Page 101, Exercise 3.

50

Past simple: regular verbs

Positive (infinitive + -ed)
I present**ed** the business plan last week.
She email**ed** the report yesterday.

*Questions (**did** + subject + infinitive)*
Did you **receive** my email yesterday?
What **did** they **discuss** at the meeting last week?

*Negative (**didn't** + infinitive)*
I **didn't talk** to Jenny.
She **didn't phone**.

···› **Grammar reference 23**

f   Can you complete these questions that Hanna asks?

1   when / you / arrive ?
When did you arrive?

2   where / you / stay ?

3   you / talk about the cost of materials ?

4   you / visit the factory ?

g   ▶▶ 89   Check your answers. Listen and repeat.

h   Make sentences about Martin's trip. Practise saying the sentences with a partner.

Martin didn't work on Thursday.

1   Martin / work / Thursday   ✗
2   he / arrive / evening   ✓
3   he / talk about / plan   ✓
4   Pedro / talk a lot   ✗
5   he / visit / factory   ✗
6   look at / production line   ✗
7   stay / Socorro Hotel   ✓
8   Miguel / phone him / yesterday   ✗

i   Grammar practice ···› Page 101, Exercise 4.

2   ▶▶ 90   PRONUNCIATION Listen and repeat these verbs in the past simple. How do we say the -ed ending? Fill in the chart.

phoned   talked   presented   received looked   visited   emailed   needed discussed   worked   stayed   started finished   travelled

/d/	/t/	/ɪd/
phoned	*talked*	*presented*

3   Communication practice 23. Student A ···› Page 83. Student B ···› Page 91.

4   Talk to a partner. When did you last:

- work late?
- stay in a hotel?
- use a fax machine?
- travel by train?
- visit a client?
- travel abroad?

USEFUL LANGUAGE

I talked to Ken and Gloria at the meeting yesterday.
We talked about the business plan.
Did you discuss the targets?
I presented the new product at the meeting.
We didn't look at the new price list.

8.3	Talking about holidays	GRAMMAR	Past simple: irregular verbs
		VOCABULARY	Holiday and travel language

1 a Match the groups of words to the photos from a holiday brochure. Use a dictionary to help you. Write 1–5 in the boxes.

1 plane | ferry | bus | coach |
2 beach | pool | sunbathe |
3 bars | restaurants | discos |
4 apartment | hotel | campsite |
5 rent a car | travel around | go sightseeing |

a
Accommodation

b
1 Transport

c
Relaxing

d
Things to do

e
Nightlife

b ▶▶ **91** Listen to Hanna Day talking to her colleague, Steven Croft, about his holiday on the Greek island of Crete. Tick (✓) the correct answer: a, b, or both.

1 He travelled to Crete by …
a plane. ✓   b ferry. ✓

2 On Crete, he stayed in …
a a hotel. ☐   b an apartment. ☐

3 There were lots of …
a bars. ☐   b restaurants. ☐

4 He travelled around by …
a car. ☐   b bus. ☐

c Vocabulary practice ···▶ Page 101, Exercise 5.

d ▶▶ **92** PRONUNCIATION Listen and match the words to the correct stress marks. Then listen again and repeat.

1 campsite   a **Ooo**
2 apartment   b **oO**
3 accommodation   c **Oo**
4 sightseeing   d **oOo**
5 hotel   e **oooOo**

2 a ▶▶ **93** Listen to sentences from the conversation in 1b. Match the sentences (1–12) to the irregular verbs you hear (a–l).

1 *h*   5 ☐   9 ☐
2 ☐   6 ☐   10 ☐
3 ☐   7 ☐   11 ☐
4 ☐   8 ☐   12 ☐

a ate b bought c came d cost e drank
f drove g flew h had i left j saw
k took l went

b Can you write the infinitives of the verbs in a–l?

a _____*eat*_____   b _____   c _____
d _____   e _____   f _____
g _____   h _____   i _____
j _____   k _____   l _____

Past simple: irregular verbs

The past simple form of some verbs is irregular. You need to learn them.

See the list of irregular verbs on page 115.

c Grammar practice ···> Page 102, Exercise 6.

3 **Look at the receipts and papers from Steven's trip. Ask and answer questions with a partner.**

A When / What / Where / How (much) did he ...?

B He ... .

4 Communication practice 24. Student A ···> Page 83. Student B ···> Page 91.

5 **Talk about past holidays with a partner.**

Where / What / How did ...?

USEFUL LANGUAGE

Did you fly or did you take the ferry?

I rented a car, and travelled around.

We went sightseeing.

I had a week relaxing and sunbathing on the beach.

We didn't stay at a hotel. We were on a campsite.

What was the nightlife like? Were the bars and restaurants OK?

AIR CANADA

Flight	From	To	Date	Depart	Arrive
AC136	Vancouver (BC)	Toronto Pearson (ON)	May 5	06:00	13:27
AC872	Toronto Pearson (ON)	Frankfurt (FRA)	May 5	17:15	07:00
AC9206	Frankfurt (FRA)	Athens (ATH)	May 6	09:05	12:50
AC9201	Athens (ATH)	Frankfurt (FRA)	May 20	06:15	
AC873	Frankfurt (FRA)	Toronto Pearson (ON)	May 2		
	(BC)		May 2		

MOS HOTEL ATHENS

Bill No. 1897465 Room No. 108
Name: Steven Croft   Nationality: Canadian
Arrival date: May 6   Departure date: May 8

SNACK HQ

** TORONTO PEARSON AIRPORT **

1 CHICKEN SANDWICH	$6.80
1 MINERAL WATER	$2.40
TOTAL:	$9.20

HELLENIC SEAWAYS

Ferry: Athens (Piraeus) – Crete (Chania)

May 8   Dep. Athens 15:45   Arr. Crete 20:15

May 19   Dep. Chania 20:45   Arr. Athens 01:15 next day

CT Coaches
Sightseeing Tours

Tour date: May 14

FAST LANE TAXIS
Receipt

VANCOUVER AIRPORT
MAY 5 $38

Sara Restaurant

MAY 11TH – 9.10 P.M. YOUR ORDER:

9 | Communication

1 **a** **Can you match the words to the documents?**

> agenda   bar chart   graph   minutes
> pie chart   schedule   table

1 *bar chart*   2 ....   3 ....
4 ....   5 ....   6 ....
7 ....

b ▶▶ **94** **Check your answers. Listen and repeat.**

c Vocabulary practice ···> Page 102, Exercise 1.

d **Read the emails and answer the questions.**

1 Why is Carla sending documents to Tim?
2 How many documents are attached in Carla's email?
3 Does Tim have a copy of the minutes?
4 Who has copies of the schedule for the new warehouse?

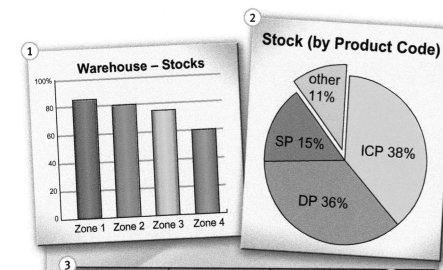

1 Warehouse – Stocks (bar chart: Zone 1, Zone 2, Zone 3, Zone 4)

2 Stock (by Product Code) (pie chart: other 11%, SP 15%, ICP 38%, DP 36%)

3

Customer	Product Code	Export	
Amati Moda	DP	Yes	
Anston Fabrics	ICP	No	
Aquarius	ICP	Yes	

4 Total Stock (graph: 27,000 to 29,000; 1–29)

5

Warehouse Zone 5 Design Phase	Feb	Mar	Apr	May
Design				
Consultation				
Revisions				
Final design				

6 Points to discuss at the meeting:
1) Warehouse Zone 5
2) Stock information

7 1) Paul Todd presented the stock forecast. All participants accepted the figures.
2) Alice Draper presented the plans for the Zone 5 project.

a

Dear Tim,

Please find attached the agenda for the meeting next Tuesday. I also attach other information you need for the meeting: a pie chart of products, a bar chart of stocks in the warehouse, a graph of stocks for last month, and a table of customers.

Alex wrote the minutes for the last meeting – I think he sent them to you.
But if you don't have them, just ask him to email you a copy.

Best regards,

Carla

b

Dear Carla,

Many thanks for the information. I read all the attachments this morning. I saw Alex yesterday, and he gave me the minutes. But I don't have a copy of the schedule for the new warehouse. Alex told me he thought you had the schedule. Could you send it to me?

Regards,

Tim

c

Tim,

I'm afraid I don't have the schedule. But I spoke to Alice Draper, the project engineer, and she said she's bringing copies to the meeting for all of us. She wants to give a presentation about the project, and she'd like to talk about the schedule then. But if you need a copy before the meeting, you can contact her. Her email address is draper@bc-structures.com.

Carla

Object pronouns

He sent **her** five documents. She read **them**.

I › me   you › you   he › him   she › her
it › it   we › us   they › them

···› **Grammar reference 24**

e Look at the grammar box. Then read the phrases 1–7 and find them in the emails (highlighted). Who or what do the underlined words refer to? Choose from these people or things.

> Alex   Tim   Carla   Alice   the minutes
> the schedule

1 ... he sent <u>them</u> to you. (them = _the minutes_)
2 ... ask <u>him</u> to email you a copy. (him = _____)
3 ... ask him to email <u>you</u> a copy. (you = _____)
4 ... he gave <u>me</u> the minutes. (me = _____)
5 Could you send <u>it</u> to me? (it = _____)
6 ... she's bringing copies to the meeting for all of <u>us</u>.
   (us = _____ , _____ , _____ and
   _____)
7 ... you can contact <u>her</u>. (her = _____)

f Grammar practice ···› Page 102, Exercise 2.

2 **a** Read the emails again. Find the past simple form of these irregular verbs.

1 give _gave_
2 have _____
3 read _____
4 say _____
5 see _____
6 send _____
7 speak _____
8 tell _____
9 think _____
10 write _____

b ▶▶ 95 Check your answers. Listen and repeat.

c Grammar practice ···› Page 102, Exercise 3.

3 Communication practice 25 ···› Page 84. Work with a partner.

USEFUL LANGUAGE

I attach the minutes of the meeting.
Please find attached my report of the trip.
I can't read the attachment.
Could you send me the schedule?
Many thanks for your message.

GRAMMAR	*will*: spontaneous decisions and offers
VOCABULARY	Telephone expressions

1 a Do you or your colleagues speak English on the telephone? Who do you speak to?

b Complete the questionnaire. Tick (✓) the boxes.

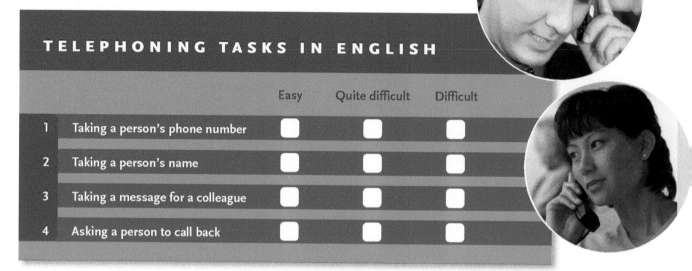

TELEPHONING TASKS IN ENGLISH

		Easy	Quite difficult	Difficult
1	Taking a person's phone number	☐	☐	☐
2	Taking a person's name	☐	☐	☐
3	Taking a message for a colleague	☐	☐	☐
4	Asking a person to call back	☐	☐	☐

c Work with a partner. Talk about your answers.

d ▶▶ **96** Listen to a woman phoning the reception at APC Ltd. Answer the questions.

1 Does the receptionist take a message?

2 Does he take the woman's name?

3 Does he take her phone number?

4 Does he ask her to call back?

e ▶▶ **96** Listen again. Complete the message.

MESSAGE

FOR ANDRÉ THOMAS:

_____

_____

_____

_____

---

2 a ▶▶ **97** Listen to three telephone calls. Are these sentences true (T) or false (F)?

Call 1 1 Louise is out of the office. ☐ F

2 Rob says he'll call Louise back. ☐

Call 2 3 Rob leaves a message. ☐

4 Rob leaves his phone number. ☐

Call 3 5 Louise phones Rob's extension. ☐

6 Rob thanks Louise for her call. ☐

b Fill in the gaps to complete the telephone calls.

> afraid   busy   calling   could   hold
> moment   back   speaking   who's

Call 1

Reception Hello. Camden Marketing.

Rob Hello. ¹ *Could* I speak to Louise Miller, please?

Reception ² _____ calling, please?

Rob Rob Sears.

Reception Her line's ³ _____ at the moment.

Rob Oh, right. Um ... OK. I'll call back later.

Reception OK.

Rob Bye.

Reception Bye.

Call 2

Reception	Hello. Camden Marketing.
Rob	Hello. Louise Miller, please. It's Rob Sears.
Reception	One ⁴_____ , please. I'm ⁵_____ she's still on the phone. Would you like to ⁶_____ ?
Rob	Um ... Could you ask her to call me back?
Reception	Yes.
Rob	She has my number.
Reception	Could I take your name again?
Rob	Yeah. Rob Sears. S-E-A-R-S.
Reception	OK. I'll ask her to call you ⁷_____ .
Rob	It's quite urgent.
Reception	OK. I'll give her the message as soon as possible.
Rob	OK. Thanks very much. Bye.
Reception	Bye.

Call 3

Rob	Hello.
Louise	Hello. Is that Rob?
Rob	Yes, ⁸_____ .
Louise	Hi, Rob. It's Louise.
Rob	Oh hi, Louise. Thanks for ⁹_____ back.
Louise	You're welcome. What can I do for you?

c ▶▶ **97** Listen to the telephone calls again. Check your answers.

d ▶▶ **98** Listen and repeat the sentences. Then, in pairs, practise the conversations in 2b.

1 Who's calling, please?
2 Her line's busy at the moment.
3 One moment, please.
4 Would you like to hold?
5 A Is that Rob?
  B Yes, speaking.
6 Thanks for calling back.

e Vocabulary practice ⋯▸ Page 102, Exercise 4.

3 **a** **Complete these sentences from the conversations in 2b.**

Call 1 (1 _____ _____ back later.)

Call 2 (2 _____ _____ her to call you back.)

(3 _____ _____ her the message as soon as possible.)

b ▶▶ **99** **Listen and repeat the sentences in 3a.**

will: *spontaneous decisions and offers*

I'll give her the message.
She'll call you back.
(I'll = I will)

Note: We use the short form ('ll) when we speak.

⋯▸ **Grammar reference 25**

c Grammar practice ⋯▸ Page 102, Exercise 5.

4 Communication practice 26. Student A ⋯▸ Page 84. Student B ⋯▸ Page 92.

USEFUL LANGUAGE

Who's calling, please?
It's Eric Blanc.
Is that Tom?
Yes, speaking.
Could I speak to Ann, please?
Sorry, I'm afraid she's out.
Can I / Could you take a message?
I'll give him the message.
Could you ask her to call me (back)?
I'll call back later.
Could I take your name?
Her line's busy at the moment.
Would you like to hold?

9.3 | Talking about the weather and climate

GRAMMAR Review of present and past tenses

VOCABULARY The weather

Manila

Milan

Moscow

1

a Read the emails (a–c) from three colleagues. What subjects do they write about?

b Read the emails again. Use a dictionary to help you. One person lives in Manila, one lives in Milan and one lives in Moscow. Which person is from which city?

1 .... is from Manila.

2 .... is from Milan.

3 .... is from Moscow.

c Look at the pictures of different types of weather. Find words in the emails to fill in the gaps.

1 It's s *unny* .

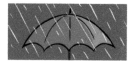

2 It's r................... .

3 It's c................... .

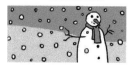

4 It's s................... .

5 It's f................... .

6 It's w................... .

7 It's f................... .

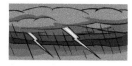

8 a t................... .

d ▶▶ **100** Check your answers. Listen and repeat.

---

a 〇〇〇

Dear Celia and Alex,

I hope you had a good weekend. I wanted to take the kids to the park, but the weather was miserable. It was cold (two degrees) and foggy all day on Saturday, then it rained all day on Sunday. Typical weather for the season. And now I'm back at work, it's a beautiful sunny day!

What's the weather like with you? Are you both OK for the conference call later today?

Seb

b 〇〇〇

Hi Seb,

Yes, I'm OK for the call. It's cloudy here this morning, and it's raining a bit. It's very hot and humid, though. It looks like we'll get a thunderstorm. I'm actually pleased to be in a cool office, with air-conditioning! The system in my apartment isn't working.

Celia

c 〇〇〇

I don't have air-conditioning at home either, Celia. But it's minus 18 degrees here at the moment, so it's not a problem! It's quite windy as well, so it feels even colder. Seb, you said it was 'cold' on Saturday (two degrees). Here, when the temperature's about zero and it's snowing, people say it's 'warm'! I guess two degrees is 'absolutely freezing' for you, Celia!

I look forward to the conference call later.

Alex

e Now find words in the emails with the same meaning as 1–5.

1 very nice = b_eautiful_
2 horrible = m_____
3 quite hot = w_____
4 quite cold = c_____
5 one below zero = m_____ one

f ▶▶ **101** Check your answers. Listen and repeat.

g Vocabulary practice ⋯> Page 103, Exercise 6.

2 a ▶▶ **102** Nigel Baker is on a business trip in France. He's having lunch with his colleague, Olivier Menard. Listen to their conversation, then answer the questions.

1 What's the weather like today?
2 What city are the colleagues in?
3 What's the Mistral?
4 What's the weather like in London today?

b Complete these sentences from the conversation. Put the verbs in the correct tense.

1 It __rained__ nearly every day last week. (rain)
2 You sometimes _____ one or two wet days. (get)
3 The sun _____ today, that's the main thing. (shine)
4 The waiter _____ with our bottle of water. (come)
5 I _____ here once before, about two years ago. (come)
6 Before, when I lived in Paris, I always _____ winter. (hate)
7 We _____ a cold wind, sometimes. (get)
8 Apparently, it _____ there at the moment. (rain)

c ▶▶ **102** Listen to the conversation again and check your answers.

> **Review of present and past tenses**
>
> *Present continuous*
> It's raining at the moment.
>
> *Present simple*
> It rains a lot in winter.
>
> *Past simple*
> It rained yesterday.

d Grammar practice ⋯> Page 103, Exercise 7.

3 Communication practice 27 ⋯> Page 84. Work with a partner.

4 a Talk about the weather in your country/ region.

What's the weather like today?
What was it like yesterday?
What's the weather usually like in:
January? April? August?

b Talk about your past experiences of extreme weather:

● very hot weather
● very cold weather
● heavy snow
● heavy rain
● strong winds

> **USEFUL LANGUAGE**
>
> *The climate*
> It rains a lot in the UK in April.
> It's often foggy in November.
>
> *The weather now*
> It's freezing.
> It's snowing.
>
> *The weather in the past*
> It rained last night.
> It was windy yesterday.

10 Progress

GRAMMAR Comparatives

VOCABULARY Comparing products and services

Airbus A380

Boeing 747

Airbus A380 or Boeing 747? The BIG question

In the 20th Century, planes got bigger, and flew faster, further and higher. But today, a new word is in the air: 'cheaper'. What does this mean for planes in the 21st Century, and for the two big companies that make them: Airbus and Boeing?

On paper, an easy way to make the cost of flying lower is to build bigger planes. One large plane with, say, 400 seats, is less expensive to fly than two smaller ones with 200 seats. This was why, in 1969, Boeing built its first 747 Jumbo Jet, for 400 passengers. Boeing's more modern Jumbo, the 747-400, still has good sales today. But is it economical to build a

plane bigger than the 747? This is a more difficult question. Because of the high costs, the development of new planes is a dangerous business.

Airbus thinks bigger is better, and is spending billions of euros on its new A380 Super Jumbo, with 550 seats. But Boeing thinks its 747 still has a future, and doesn't want to spend billions of dollars on a new, larger model. Large planes are a big percentage of both firms' business. At present, each company has about 50% of the world market for passenger planes. If the A380 is safe, reliable and more economical than the 747, then Airbus can become the market leader. But if the first A380 has serious technical problems or, worse, safety problems, then the future of the Super Jumbo – and the future of Airbus – is in question.

---

1 a **Read the article. Use a dictionary to help you. Then <u>underline</u> the correct words so that the sentences are true.**

1 The Airbus A380 is a very *large*/small plane.

2 Today, the first 747s are quite *modern*/old.

3 The A380 project is *cheap*/expensive.

4 Boeing *is*/isn't building a new Super Jumbo.

5 Airbus has *half*/a third of the world market.

b **Fill in the gaps with the adjectives.**

> dangerous difficult economical easy
> expensive cheap low reliable safe

1 Airlines want ___low___ costs and passengers want _____ tickets.

2 Concorde was very fast, but cost a lot to fly. It wasn't very _____ .

3 Plane crashes are rare – flying is a very _____ way to travel.

4 In the air, technical problems are _____ .

5 Passengers want to arrive on time – they want a _____ service.

6 New planes are _____ . They cost billions of dollars to develop.

7 Planes are _____ to land when it's very windy.

8 Computers help to make a lot of jobs quite _____ for pilots.

c Vocabulary practice ···> Page 103, Exercise 1.

2 **a** **Fill in the gaps. Choose from these words.**

> cheaper   easier   larger   lower
> more/less dangerous
> more/less economical
> more/less difficult
> more/less expensive

1 It's less expensive. = It's _cheaper_ .
2 It's bigger. = It's _____ .
3 The cost is higher. = It's _____
    _____ .
4 It's safer. = It's _____ _____ .
5 It's less difficult. = It's _____ .
6 It costs less to use. = It's _____
    _____ .

b ▶▶ **103** **Check your answers. Listen and repeat.**

c **Write the irregular comparatives for these adjectives. You can find them in the text.**

1 (+) far _____   2 (+) good _____
3 (+) bad _____

d ▶▶ **104** **Check your answers. Listen and repeat.**

> *Comparatives*
>
> Short adjectives
> cheap › cheap**er**
> fast › fast**er**
>
> *Long adjectives*
> (+) difficult › **more** difficult
> (–) expensive › **less** expensive
>
> *Irregular adjectives*
> good › **better**
> bad › **worse**
> far › **further**
>
> **than**
> The Airbus A380 is **bigger than** the Boeing 747.
>
> ···> **Grammar reference 26**

e **Grammar practice** ···> **Page 103, Exercise 2.**

f **Make sentences using comparatives.**

1 the Airbus A380 / large / the Boeing 747 .
   The Airbus A380 is larger than the Boeing 747.
2 the 747-400 / modern / the first 747 .
   ....
3 modern planes / economical / older ones .
   ....
4 air travel / safe / road travel .
   ....
5 flying a plane / difficult / driving a car .
   ....
6 because of computers, modern planes / easy / fly .
   ....

g **Work with a partner. Compare these products.**

Mini

Porsche

3 **a** ▶▶ **105** **Shelley Spears works for the airline JetNet. Listen to her giving a presentation to her colleagues. What are the advantages and disadvantages of economy class? Make notes in the chart.**

Advantages	Disadvantages

b **Can you add anymore advantages/disadvantages to the chart?**

4 **Communication practice 28** ···> **Page 85. Work with a partner.**

> USEFUL LANGUAGE
>
> Planes are safer now than they were.
> The new model is more economical, but I think it's less reliable.
> Ticket sales are better/worse than last year.
> The disadvantage is the higher cost.
> The advantage is that it's cheaper.

1 **a** **Read the article. Circle the correct answers.**

1 Ryanair is:
   a a large airline
   (b) a low-cost airline.

2 Where's there most competition between airlines?
   a long flights
   b short flights

3 What's an advantage of low-cost airlines?
   a cheap fares
   b big meals

4 Some people prefer high-speed trains because they are:
   a cheap
   b convenient

5 Seats in TGV trains are:
   a comfortable
   b small

b **Complete the sentences with superlatives. Use the article to help you.**

1 __*The safest*__ way to travel is by plane. *(safe)*

2 The TGV is _____ train in Europe. *(fast)*

3 Air France-KLM is _____ airline in Europe. *(large)*

4 People often want to buy _____ tickets. *(cheap)*

5 Some people want _____ way to travel. *(convenient)*

6 Low-cost airlines often have _____ fares. *(expensive)*

7 _____ seats are in first class. *(good)*

The European Transport Race:
Quick Packets of Peanuts and High-Speed Cows

If big planes are the safest way to travel, big airlines are not the safest businesses. In Europe, the largest companies, Air France-KLM, British Airways and Lufthansa, are finding it difficult to make money from shorter flights. The problem is competition – in the air, and on the ground.

Low-cost airlines, such as Ryanair and easyJet, are winning more and more customers on short European routes. Most flights in Europe are less than 1,000 km, so there's a lot of business to win – and lose. Low-cost airlines often don't fly to the nearest airports to big cities, but their passengers are happy to travel further out of town to get the cheapest fares. And when they pay peanuts for their

c **▶▶ 106** **Listen and check your answers.**

Superlatives

Short adjectives	*Long adjectives*	*Irregular adjectives*
the cheap**est**	**the most** expensive	good › **the best**
the fast**est**	**the least** convenient	bad › **the worst**

···> Grammar reference 27

d **Grammar practice ···> Page 103, Exercise 3.**

tickets, customers are also happy to have a quick snack from a packet, or no food at all, instead of an in-flight meal.

There's competition on the ground, too. People who want the most convenient journey, rather than the least expensive fare, often find high-speed trains are the best way to travel. Europe's fastest train, the French TGV, is the quickest way to get from city centre to city centre on many routes. There are now international TGV lines between Paris, London, Brussels and Cologne, and there are plans for new routes and faster lines. Compared with most planes, the TGV also has bigger, more comfortable seats – better for working, or watching cows go past at 300 km/h.

b ▶▶ **108** **Listen and repeat these sentences from the conversation.**

1 I agree.
2 That's true.
3 I'm not so sure.
4 I prefer to fly.
5 You're right.
6 I think it's the worst way to travel.

c Vocabulary practice ⋯> Page 103, Exercise 4.

3 Communication practice 29 ⋯> Page 85.
Work with a partner.

4 Compare travelling by plane, train and car. What are the advantages and disadvantages? Give your opinion for each of these situations.

- a one-day business trip to another city
- a week at a conference in another city
- a holiday abroad

2 a ▶▶ **107** **Listen to two businesspeople talking on a plane. They're discussing ways of travelling from Paris to Frankfurt. Do they agree (A) or disagree (D)? Write A or D in the boxes.**

1 Flying is always the fastest.   A
2 The train is the most convenient.   ☐
3 The train is the cheapest.   ☐
4 Driving is the worst.   ☐

USEFUL LANGUAGE

I think this is the best way to travel.
Yes, I agree.
I think you're right.
I'm not so sure.
I prefer to go by train.
This is the cheapest option.
Yes, that's true.
What do you think?
It's a question of cost.

10.3 | Checking in for a flight

GRAMMAR	Countable and uncountable nouns *some/any/no*
VOCABULARY	Airport language

1 a Look at the airport screen. Complete the sentences with words from the screen.

1 The flights to ___*New York*___ , _____ and _____ aren't late. They're _____ .

2 The flight to _____ is late. It's _____ by 30 minutes.

3 You can check in now for the flight to _____ . The check-in is _____ .

4 You can't check in for the flight to _____ . The check-in is _____ .

5 There's no flight to _____ . It's _____ .

6 For the flight to _____ , go to _____ D10.

7 The passengers are getting on the plane to _____ now. They're _____ .

b ▶▶ 109 Listen and check your answers.

TERMINAL 2 – DEPARTURES   Time: 11:16

FLIGHT NUMBER	DESTINATION	SCHEDULED DEPARTURE	GATE	INFORMATION
	Tokyo Narita	11:15	E10	Delayed – expected 11:45
	New York JFK	11:30	D15	On time – boarding
	London Heathrow	11:40	D18	On time – check-in closed
	Los Angeles Int'l	12:10	D10	On time – check-in open
	Singapore Changi	12:30	E22	Cancelled

2 a ▶▶ 110 Listen to a passenger checking in for a flight. Answer the questions.

1 What identification does the man have?

2 Does he get a window seat?

3 Why is the plane full?

4 Is the flight on time?

5 Does the man have any luggage to check in?

6 Which gate does he need to go to?

7 Where are the shops?

b **Fill in the gaps in the travel vocabulary.**

| aisle boarding brief card case |
| hand seat |

1 identity _card_

2 window _____

3 _____ seat

4 _____ luggage

5 suit_____

6 _____case

7 _____ pass

c **▶▶ 110 Listen to the conversation in 2a again and check your answers. Then practise saying the words in 1–7.**

d Vocabulary practice ···▷ Page 104, Exercise 5.

e **Work with a partner. Can you count these things or not? Write the words in the chart.**

| suitcase luggage ticket identification |
| identity card information |

Countable a/an (plural = some)	Uncountable some (no plural)
suitcase	luggage

f **▶▶ 110 Listen to the conversation again. <u>Underline</u> the words you hear in these sentences.**

1 Do you have *some/<u>any</u>/no* identification?

2 I'm afraid there are *some/any/no* window seats left.

3 Do you have *some/any/no* luggage?

4 So you have *some/any/no* luggage to check in.

5 No, I don't have *some/any/no* other bags.

6 Are there *some/any/no* shops after the security check?

7 There are *some/any/no* shops over there.

---

some/any/no

Questions: **any**
Do you have **any** information about the flight?

Positive sentences: **some**
There are **some** passengers at the check-in.

Negative sentences:
no or *negative verb* + **any**
I have **no** hand luggage.
I **don't** have **any** hand luggage.

···▷ **Grammar reference 28 and 33**

g Grammar practice ···▷ Page 104, Exercise 6.

3 Communication practice 30. Student A ···▷ Page 85. Student B ···▷ Page 92.

4 **Talk about your bad or funny experiences of travelling by plane.**

- delays
- cancellations
- lost luggage
- missing a flight
- forgetting your ticket or passport

USEFUL LANGUAGE

Is the flight on time?

No, it's delayed. It's 40 minutes late.

There's no flight to Jakarta today. It's cancelled.

The flight is boarding now, at gate B9.

Would you like an aisle seat or a window seat?

Do you have any luggage to check in?

Only hand luggage.

Here's your boarding pass.

11 | Plans

1 **a** ▶▶ **111** **Kristi Cortland is phoning her colleague, Akio Soga, in Tokyo. Listen to their conversation and fill in the gaps.**

Kristi So, where shall we meet?

Akio Um ... well, I can come to your office, or you can come here.

Kristi Well, you came here last time, so ¹ _shall_ I ² _____ to Tokyo?

Akio Yes, OK. Yeah, then you can meet our new design manager.

Kristi Oh, yes. Good idea. OK, so ³ _____ ⁴ _____ in Tokyo.

Akio OK. How many days do we need?

Kristi Hmm ... good question.

Akio ⁵ _____ we ⁶ _____ the meeting, first? Then we can decide when to meet, and how long we need ...

Kristi Yes, OK.

Akio I wrote a list, this morning, of the things I'd like to look at with you.

Kristi Right. Good.

Akio So, um ... well, ⁷ _____ I ⁸ _____ it to you? Then you can look at it, and we can talk later.

Kristi Yes, OK, good idea. ⁹ _____ ¹⁰ _____ that.

Akio I'll send it now. And I'll call back, um ... When ¹¹ _____ I ¹² _____ you?

Kristi ¹³ _____ ¹⁴ _____ again in an hour.

Akio OK, fine. Bye.

b ▶▶ **112** **Listen and repeat the sentences.**

1 Shall we plan the meeting?
2 Where shall we meet?
3 Shall I come to Tokyo?
4 When shall I call you?
5 Let's talk again.
6 Let's do that.

Making suggestions

Shall + I/we + *infinitive*
Shall we meet next month?
Shall I call tomorrow?
Where **shall** we meet?
When **shall** I phone you?

Let's + *infinitive*
Let's go now.
Let's meet next week.
(Let**'s** = Let **us**)

···> **Grammar reference 29**

c Grammar practice ···> Page 104, Exercise 1.

d Work with a partner. Make suggestions about these things:

- go for lunch
- meet tomorrow
- talk next week
- discuss this now
- decide later
- put on the agenda

2 **a** ▶▶ **113** Listen to Kristi and Akio planning their meeting. Put the jobs in the correct order. Write 1–5 in the boxes.

☐		
1	a	Start work on the sales brochure.
↓		
☐	b	Check the prices.
↓		
☐	c	Choose the photos.
↓		
☐	d	Talk about new products.
↓		
☐	e	Look at the website design.

b ▶▶ **113** Listen again. Are these sentences true (T) or false (F)?

1 It's important to work on the brochure. ☐ T
2 Choosing the photos is quite urgent. ☐
3 The website design is a small job. ☐
4 Talking about new products is very urgent. ☐

c ▶▶ **114** PRONUNCIATION Listen and repeat. <u>Underline</u> the stressed word in each sentence.

1 It's <u>urgent</u>.
2 It's quite urgent.
3 It's very urgent.
4 It's important.
5 It's quite important.
6 It's very important.

d Put the words in order. Make sentences. Then put the sentences in the correct order. Write 1–4 in the boxes.

everybody / email / finally / details / to / the .
☐ *Finally, email the details to everybody.*
meeting / book / then / a / room .
☐ ....
the / of / arrange / a / all / first / date / meeting / for .
☐ ....
that / after / agenda / prepare / the .
☐ ....

e ▶▶ **115** Listen and check your answers.

f Vocabulary practice ⋯▷ Page 104, Exercise 2.

g ▶▶ **116** Listen to people agreeing and disagreeing. Fill in the gaps. Then practise the conversations with a partner.

1 **A** It's very important to check the dates.
  B Yes, I *agree* .
2 **A** The design of the brochure is a small job.
  B I'm not .... about that.
3 **A** I think you're the best person for the job.
  B I'm sorry , I .... agree.
4 **A** Shall we call to find out the latest figures?
  B That's a good ....

3 Communication practice 31 ⋯▷ Page 86. Work with a partner.

USEFUL LANGUAGE

First, let's talk about the photos.
Then, we can discuss the design.
Next, we can talk about the website.
After that, let's discuss new products.
Shall we check the brochure before the prices?
The most important/urgent job is the brochure.

GRAMMAR Future with *going to*

VOCABULARY Objectives

> ## Future with **going to**
>
> *Positive*
> I**'m going** to discuss the plan.
> He**'s going to** talk about the project.
> They**'re going to** call the supplier.
>
> *Questions*
> **What are** you **going to** talk about at the meeting?
> **Are** you **going to** discuss the website?
>
> *Negative*
> No, we **aren't / we're not going** to talk about the website.
>
> ···> **Grammar reference 30**

d Grammar practice ···> Page 104, Exercise 3.

---

1 a ▶▶ **117** Listen to Kristi Cortland talking to her manager, Simon Mills. They're discussing Kristi's plans. Are these sentences true (T) or false (F)?

1 Kristi's going to meet Akio in Tokyo. `T`
2 They're going to work on the English brochure. ☐
3 Kristi's going to change the website. ☐
4 She's going to have the website ready next week. ☐
5 She's going to send Simon a schedule. ☐

b Can you complete the sentences from the conversation? Use the correct form of *be* + *going to*.

1 You *'re going to* meet Akio.
2 I _____ talk to Akio next week.
3 We _____ look at the website.
4 _____ you _____ show me the new site?
5 When _____ you _____ have it ready?

c ▶▶ **118** Check your answers. Listen and repeat.

---

2 a ▶▶ **117** Listen to 1a again. Fill in the gaps in the extracts.

Extract 1

Kristi Er … we're going to look at the website, as well.
Simon Right. I wanted to ask you about that. What's the ¹ *plan* for the website, exactly?
Kristi Well, I want to change the design. Um …
Simon Completely?
Kristi I think we need to make some big changes, yes.
Simon Why? What's the … what's the ² _____ ?
Kristi Well, we need to make it easier to use. Um … that's the main ³ _____ .
Simon Right.

Extract 2

Simon OK, good. When are you going to have it ready? What's your ⁴ _____ date?
Kristi Well, our ⁵ _____ is to have the new site online this year … before the end of the year. … That's our ⁶ _____ .

b Look at the transcript for 1a on page 125 and check your answers.

c Vocabulary practice ⋯› Page 105, Exercise 4.

3 **a** Read the emails. Where and when are Kristi and Akio going to meet?

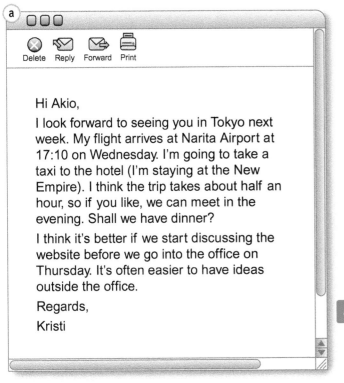

Hi Akio,

I look forward to seeing you in Tokyo next week. My flight arrives at Narita Airport at 17:10 on Wednesday. I'm going to take a taxi to the hotel (I'm staying at the New Empire). I think the trip takes about half an hour, so if you like, we can meet in the evening. Shall we have dinner?

I think it's better if we start discussing the website before we go into the office on Thursday. It's often easier to have ideas outside the office.

Regards,

Kristi

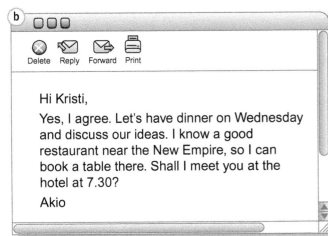

Hi Kristi,

Yes, I agree. Let's have dinner on Wednesday and discuss our ideas. I know a good restaurant near the New Empire, so I can book a table there. Shall I meet you at the hotel at 7.30?

Akio

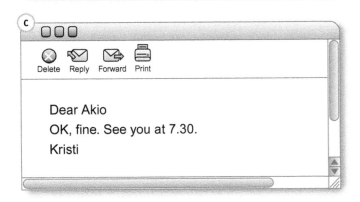

Dear Akio

OK, fine. See you at 7.30.

Kristi

b Read the emails again. Then make sentences about Kristi's plans. Use *going to*.

1 Kristi / at Narita airport.
   Kristi's going to arrive at Narita Airport.

2 She / to the hotel.
   ----

3 She / at the New Empire Hotel.
   ----

4 Kristi and Akio / on Wednesday evening.
   ----

5 They / dinner.
   ----

6 They / their ideas.
   ----

7 Akio / a table at the restaurant.
   ----

8 They / at the hotel at 7.30.
   ----

4 **a** What are your plans for next week? Write five things you're going to do.

I'm going to -------------------------------

----

b Work in pairs. Ask about your partner's plans for next week. Take it in turns.

A What are you going to do next week?

B On ... I'm going to ... .

5 Communication practice 32 ⋯› Page 86. Work with a partner.

USEFUL LANGUAGE

We're going to discuss the project next week.
What's the plan/objective?
Our aim/target/goal is to finish the work today.

1 **a** ▶▶ **119** Listen to Kristi Cortland checking into a hotel in Tokyo. Fill in the gaps with numbers.

1 Kristi is staying for _3_ nights.

2 She's in room ....

3 Breakfast is from .... am.

4 The number for room service is ....

5 Akio Soga is coming at .... pm.

b ▶▶ **119** Listen again. Are these sentences true (T) or false (F)?

1 Kristi is in a double room.   ☐ F

2 She fills in a form.   ☐

3 She knows the account number.   ☐

4 She needs to sign the form.   ☐

5 The receptionist gives her a key.   ☐

6 She wants a wake-up call.   ☐

c ▶▶ **119** Listen again to the conversation. What does Kristi need to write on the form?

....

....

d Now look at the transcript on page 126. Can you change 1–5 to make sentences from the conversation? Use *have got*.

1 I have a reservation.
   I've got a reservation.

2 Do you have a pen?
   ....

3 I don't have the number.
   ....

4 We have 24-hour room service.
   ....

5 You have a message from Mr Soga.
   ....

e ▶▶ **120** Check your answers. Listen and repeat.

have got

Positive
I**'ve got** a credit card.
He**'s got** a message.

Negative
We **haven't got** a reservation.
She **hasn't got** a key.

Questions
Have you **got** his number?
Has the hotel **got** a restaurant?

···> Grammar reference 31

f Grammar practice ···> Page 105, Exercise 5.

2 **a** ▶▶ 121 **Kristi is at the hotel reception desk. Listen to her conversation and fill in the gaps.**

Kristi	'Morning. Could I check ¹ *out* , please?
Reception	Certainly. Room three one five.
Kristi	My company's paying the ² _____ . I just have to pay the ³ _____ .
Reception	OK. So, one phone ⁴ _____ .
Kristi	Yes. And some orange juice from the ⁵ _____ .
Reception	Yes. That's all. OK. So ⁶ _____ one thousand five hundred and fifty yen, please.
Kristi	Can I pay by ⁷ _____ card?
Reception	Of course.
Kristi	⁸ _____ you are.
Reception	Thank you.

b Vocabulary practice ···> Page 105, Exercise 6.

c ▶▶ 122 **PRONUNCIATION Listen and repeat. Try to use the same intonation.**

1 Could you fill in this form, please?

2 Would you like a wake-up call?

3 Could I check out, please?

4 Can I pay by credit card?

d **Practise the conversation from 2a in pairs. Change roles.**

3 Communication practice 33. Student A ···> Page 86. Student B ···> Page 92.

4 **Talk about your best and worst experiences of staying in hotels. Why were they good or bad?**

USEFUL LANGUAGE

Checking into a hotel
I've got a reservation.

  single
A double room.
  twin

Could you fill in this form, please?
Can you sign this?
Put your signature here.
Here's the key for your room.
Would you like a wake-up call?

Checking out of a hotel
Could I check out, please?
My company's paying the bill.
I just have to pay the extras.
I had some orange juice from the minibar.
Can I pay by credit card?

Toreador Sports
Third quarter results 'on track'

The sports clothing and equipment store, Toreador, reported good third quarter results today.
The company's profit increased by 38% on the second quarter. Mervin Clay, the chief executive, said Toreador is 'on the right track'.

MR CLAY SAID, 'When I came here two years ago, I had one objective – stop ¹*making / losing* money and start making a ²*profit / loss*. My first goal was to improve business in the stores we had. We stopped opening new stores, we worked hard to ³*increase / decrease* sales and cut costs. And we did that quickly. Today, we have ⁴*higher / lower costs*, ⁵*higher / lower sales*, and a ⁶*good / bad* profit margin. We're ⁷*making / losing* money again.

Now we can think about opening new stores. At the moment, we have no final target. Our aim is to open one new store at a time. It's better to progress slowly and make a ⁸*profit / loss*, than grow fast and ⁹*make / lose* money.

Managers make their biggest mistakes when things are going well. I'm not saying we're doing well now. But we're not doing badly. We're on the right track, and we're aiming to stay on the right track. We're not going to try to run before we can walk.'

1 **a** **Read the first paragraph of the article. Answer the questions.**

   1 What does Toreador sell?
   2 Are the company's results better or worse than before?

b **Can you complete the text? <u>Underline</u> the correct words in the article (1–9). Use a dictionary to help you.**

c ▶▶ **123 Now listen to Mervin Clay speaking at a press conference and check your answers.**

d Match the words from the article to the definitions (1–9).

> costs   decrease   improve   increase   loss
> margin   profit   quarter   sales

1 3 months = a *quarter*
2 to make money = to make a _____
3 to lose money = to make a _____
4 how much a company sells = _____
5 what a company spends = _____
6 to get better = to _____
7 % profit = profit _____
8 to go up = to _____
9 to go down = to _____

e ▶▶ 124 Check your answers. Listen and repeat.

f Vocabulary practice ⋯▸ Page 105, Exercise 1.

2 a Make true sentences about Toreador Sports. Underline the correct adverbs.

1 At the moment, Toreador is doing quite *badly/well*.
2 After Mr Clay joined the company, his people worked *badly/hard*.
3 After Mr Clay joined the company, business improved *slowly/quickly*.
4 Mr Clay thinks it's better for businesses to grow *slowly/fast*.

b ▶▶ 125 Listen and check your answers. Practise saying the adverbs in 2a.

> *Adverbs of manner*
>
> *Most adverbs of manner end in -***ly***:*
> slow › slow**ly** ›
> quick › quick**ly**
>
> *These adverbs of manner are irregular:*
> good › **well**
> hard › **hard** *(no change)*
> fast › **fast** *(no change)*
>
> ⋯▸ **Grammar reference 32**

c Grammar practice ⋯▸ Page 105, Exercise 2.

d Work in pairs. Discuss these sentences. Are they true for you?

I work hard every day.
I prefer to work slowly and quietly.
I work well in a team.
I solve problems quickly.

3 a ▶▶ 126 Listen to two store managers from Toreador Sports talking at a company conference. They're discussing how business is going. Are these sentences true (T) or false (F)?

1 At the Vienna store, business is getting better. 〔T〕
2 Last year, business was very good. ☐
3 Last year, the profit margin was low. ☐
4 Last year, both stores lost money. ☐
5 This year, costs are increasing. ☐

b ▶▶ 127 PRONUNCIATION Listen and repeat the pairs of words. Are the underlined sounds the same or different?

			the same	different
1	l<u>o</u>se	l<u>o</u>st	☐	✓
2	m<u>o</u>ney	c<u>o</u>mpany	☐	☐
3	impr<u>o</u>ve	c<u>o</u>st	☐	☐
4	pr<u>o</u>fit	pr<u>o</u>duct	☐	☐
5	sl<u>o</u>w	s<u>o</u>ld	☐	☐
6	d<u>oi</u>ng	g<u>oi</u>ng	☐	☐

4 Communication practice 34. Student A ⋯▸ Page 87. Student B ⋯▸ Page 92.

5 Talk to a partner. How's business at your company, or another company you know?

> USEFUL LANGUAGE
>
> How's business?
> We're doing well/badly at the moment.
> Sales are increasing slowly/quickly/fast.
> We made a profit/loss in the last quarter.
> We made/lost $5 million.
> Things are improving / getting worse.

1 a Read the article and answer the questions. Use a dictionary to help you.

1 Why are profit margins low in supermarkets?

2 Why do supermarkets earn a lot of interest?

3 Why can big supermarkets sell goods cheaply?

b Fill in the gaps with these words from the article.

> compete   competition   competitive
> competitors   demand   discount   goods

1 We're not the only company in the market. We have three _competitors_ .

2 A lot of people are buying the product. There's a lot of _____ for it.

3 A lot of companies sell this product, so there's a lot of _____ .

4 There are a lot of companies in the market. It's very _____ .

5 We sell the same products as them. We _____ with them.

6 Our supplier gives us a 10% _____ if we buy 2,000 products.

7 I don't know their products. What sort of _____ do they sell?

c ▶▶ 128 Check your answers. Listen and repeat.

d PRONUNCIATION Fill in the chart with the words from 1b.

O	
Oo	
oO	*demand*
oOoo	
ooOo	

e Vocabulary practice ⋯▸ Page 105, Exercise 3.

f Discuss the questions in the last paragraph of the article. What's your opinion?

Are supermarkets *super markets?*

Demand isn't a problem for supermarkets. People always need groceries. But strong demand means strong competition. And when your competitors sell the same goods as you, there's only one way to compete: sell cheaply.

Low prices mean supermarkets only earn a small margin on a lot of the goods they sell. But they have another strategy for making money – they sell products *before* they pay for them. Money from sales can earn interest in the bank for weeks, sometimes months, before stores pay their suppliers.

And supermarkets have another advantage compared with smaller shops. Because they order large quantities from suppliers, they can negotiate big discounts. So the biggest supermarkets can sell at the most competitive prices.

But are supermarkets really *super markets*? Are strong competition, big stores and big discounts always good for customers, and for the retail business?

much/many: *questions*

We use many *with things we can count (countable nouns).*

How **many** store**s**/product**s**/competitor**s** do you have?

We use much *with things we can't count (uncountable nouns).*

How **much** demand/competition/discount is there?

Note: We use much/many *in questions and negative sentences.*

···> **Grammar reference 33 and 34**

d Grammar practice ···> Page 106, Exercise 4.

3 Communication practice 35. Student A ···> Page 87. Student B ···> Page 93.

2 a ▶▶ **129** **Listen to a manager and a buyer from Toreador Sports discussing an order for some T-shirts. Complete the information.**

1 Number of products ordered: *2,500*

2 Number of stores to test the product:

....

3 Sales price in stores: ....

4 Profit margin on this order: ....%

5 Maximum discount on big orders: .... %

b **Listen again and complete the questions from the conversation. Use *much/many*.**

1 So, how *many* T-shirts did we order?

2 **B** It's a new product, so we want to test it first.

 A Sure. How .... stores are we selling them in?

3 **B** It's a cheap product.

 A Hmm. Are we making .... profit on them?

4 And what about bigger orders? How .... discount can we get?

5 **B** I think we can get a maximum 20% discount on really big orders.

 A Is there .... demand at the moment? That's the question. Do .... people want to buy T-shirts in winter?

c ▶▶ **129** **Listen again and check your answers.**

4 **Talk about a market/industry from the box (or one you know well).**

food   soft drinks   mobile
clothes/fashion

What's the biggest company in the market?
Who are the company's competitors?
Is the market very competitive?
Is demand increasing or decreasing?

USEFUL LANGUAGE

Market forces
How much competition is there? Is the market very competitive?
What companies do you compete with? Do you have many competitors?
Is there much demand at the moment?

Orders and prices
How many products did we order?
When did we order the goods?
How much discount is there?
What's the profit margin? How much do we earn on the product?

12.3	Shopping	GRAMMAR	*this/these, that/those*
		VOCABULARY	**Shopping language**

1 **a** **Discuss these questions.**

Do you have sales in your country? When are they?

In your opinion, what are the advantages/disadvantages of shopping in the sales?

b **Fill in the gaps 1–7.**

> cards   changing   free   half   off   receipt   size

SALE
EVERYTHING
1 *half*
PRICE

We accept all major credit
2 _____

SPECIAL OFFER
buy 2 get 1 3 _____

4 _____
Room

THANK YOU FOR SHOPPING
WITH US.
PLEASE KEEP YOUR
5 _____

Toreador Sportswear
6 _____
XL

50%
7 _____

c ▶▶ **130** **Check your answers. Listen and repeat.**

d **Work with a partner. Can you fill in the gaps in the sentences?**

> cash   change   cheque   extra   medium
> number   try

1 In a shop, you can pay with a credit card, with a *cheque* , or with _____ .

2 If something costs €15, and you pay with a €20 note, you get €5 _____ .

3 When you pay by credit card, you sign your name or put in a pin _____ .

4 Sizes of T-shirts are small, _____ , large and _____ large.

5 People often _____ on clothes and shoes before they buy them.

e ▶▶ **131** **Check your answers. Listen and repeat.**

f Vocabulary practice ···▶ **Page 106, Exercise 5.**

2 **a** ▶▶ 132 **Listen to five conversations between customers and shop assistants. Circle the correct answer: a, b or c.**

1 The price of the T-shirt is _____ .
   a £3.00 (b) £13.00 c £30.00
2 The UK shoe size is _____ .
   a 9½ b 10 c 10½
3 The price of the watch is _____ .
   a £95.50 b £95.90 c £99.50
4 The customer chooses _____ .
   a blue b pink c yellow
5 The customer gives a _____ .
   a signature b pin number c bank note

b ▶▶ 132 **Listen again. Fill in the gaps with *this*, *that*, *these* or *those*.**

1 A Do you need any help?
   B Yes, how much is __*this*__ T-shirt? I can't find the price on it.
   A Er ... Let's have a look. Is _____ it, there?
2 A Excuse me. I'm just looking at _____ shoes. I'm a size 45, European size. What's _____ in a UK size?
3 A ... I'd like to look at a watch, if I can, please.
   B Sure.
   A It's _____ one there, at the back.
   B _____ one here?
4 A Hello. Could I have one of _____ , please?
   B One of _____ , here? The bracelets?
5 A Can I pay with _____ credit card?
   B Yes, we accept _____ . That's fine.

c **Look at the transcript for 2a on page 127. Check your answers.**

---

this/these, that/those

Things that are very near you, or in your hand:
Singular: How much is **this** shirt?
Plural: Are **these** jeans in the sale?

Things that are further from you, that you point at:
Singular: I like **that** mobile phone.
Plural: Could I have one of **those** sandwiches, please?

···> Grammar reference 35

d ▶▶ 133 **Practise saying the sentences in the grammar box. Listen and repeat.**

e Grammar practice ···> Page 106, Exercise 6.

3 Communication practice 36 ···> Page 87. Work with a partner.

4 **a** ▶▶ 134 **Listen to two people giving their opinions about shopping. Answer the questions.**

Person 1
1 How often does she go shopping for clothes?
2 Does she buy much on shopping trips?
3 When doesn't she like shopping?

Person 2
4 Does she like shopping?
5 Does she spend a lot of money on clothes?
6 Does she buy clothes and never wear them?

b **Which of the two people is most like you?**

c **Talk about your shopping habits.**

What do/don't you like about shopping?
Do you prefer shopping alone or with someone?
Where do you like to go shopping (local shops, big shopping centres, out-of-town stores, markets)?

USEFUL LANGUAGE

I'd like to look at those bracelets.
What's that in a UK size?
I'm a size forty, European size.
Could I try it/them on?
I'll have a red/blue one, please.
Can I pay with this credit card?

Communication practice

COMMUNICATION PRACTICE 1
(1.1, EXERCISE 4)

Student A: Welcome Student B to your company. Then introduce Student B to Student C. Change roles.

Student A
Name: John/Jane Costas
Company: AMK

Student B
Name: Michael/Michelle Parker
Company: IST

Student C
Name: Christopher/Christine May
Company: EJD

COMMUNICATION PRACTICE 2
(1.2, EXERCISE 4)

Take it in turns to ask and answer where you're from. Use the cities on the maps.

A Where are you from?
B I'm ... .
A Where's ...?
B It's in ..., near ... .

COMMUNICATION PRACTICE 3
(1.3, EXERCISE 3)

Take it in turns to offer and ask for drinks.

A Would you like a drink?
B Yes, please. Could I have ... ?

COMMUNICATION PRACTICE 4
(2.1, EXERCISE 5)

Student A

Exchange numbers with Student B. Write the numbers.

A What's your ... number?
B It's ... .
A Sorry?
B It's ... .
A So, ...
B That's right.

Student A		Student B	
Tel:	0579 4567544	Tel:	
Mobile:	06344598771	Mobile:	
Fax:	0579 6670035	Fax:	
email:	p.james@ddk.uk	email:	

COMMUNICATION PRACTICE 5
(2.2, EXERCISE 4)

Take it in turns to ask for and say the time.

COMMUNICATION PRACTICE 6
(2.3, EXERCISE 5)

Practise buying snacks and drinks in a café. Take it in turns to be the customer and the assistant.

A Could I have ... , please.
B Anything else?
A No, thanks. / Yes, ...
B € ..., please.

Snacks

cheese and tomato sandwich	€3.40
egg sandwich	€3.60
tuna sandwich	€3.50
chicken sandwich	€3.60
salad	€3.90
burger	€3.70
hotdog	€3.40

Drinks

coffee	€1.90
tea	€1.80
orange juice	€1.90
mineral water	€1.60

COMMUNICATION PRACTICE 7
(3.1, EXERCISE 3)

Student A

Ask and answer questions. Fill in the chart.

Where ... live?   What ... do?   What company ... work for?   Where ... work?   How do you spell that?

	Home	Job	Company	Place
1	Moscow	manager	CTT	factory
2				
3	Berlin	technician	Beckmann	lab
4				
5	Paris	receptionist	Indigo Trade	hotel
6				

COMMUNICATION PRACTICE 8
(3.2, EXERCISE 6)

Student A

Ask and answer questions. Fill in the chart.

Where ... come from / live?   What company ... own?

Name	Comes from	Lives	Company
Ana Pons		London	
Hans Bauer	Vienna	Berlin	
Sandy Cohen		Paris	
Michael Pitt	London		TJ Foods
Claire Garnier		Zurich	
Pedro Cruz	Valencia		Electrina

COMMUNICATION PRACTICE 9
(3.3, EXERCISE 3)

Look at the example. Then make similar conversations for 1–5. Use negatives for underlined words.

I get up / 6.00.
I / early. I / 8.00.

    A I get up at six o'clock.
    B I don't get up early. I get up at eight.

1 We / coffee break / 10.00.
We / coffee breaks. The office / have / coffee machine!

2 I / morning person.
I / morning person.

3 People start work early / this country.
They / start early / my country. But / work late.
People work late / this country. We / evening people!
We / morning people!

4 My boss / finish / 8.00 pm.
My boss / work late. She finish / 5.00.

5 Sorry / late.
Late? You / late.
I / 5 minutes late.
No problem.

COMMUNICATION PRACTICE 10
(4.1, EXERCISE 4)

Student A

Read this page from a report about business on the Internet. Ask your partner questions. Find out what the words in highlight stand for/mean and complete the notes. Answer your partner's questions.

... mean?   ... stand for?   ... spell ...?
... say that again?   ... speak slowly?

Business on the Internet – Contents

Page

3   Business online   = ...

7   What is 'e-business'?   = 'electronic' business
                            = business on the Internet

11   A name for your URL   = ...

13   B2B   = business-to-business
     – business connections

17   The webmaster   = ...

20   Buy the right PC   = personal computer

COMMUNICATION PRACTICE 11
(4.2, EXERCISE 4)

Student A

Write an email to your partner (on paper). Ask for his/her phone number.

Your partner will send you an email. Write a reply.

COMMUNICATION PRACTICE 12
(4.3, EXERCISE 4)

Student A

Read about Zelton Software's website, then answer your partner's questions.

Zelton Software sells software on its website, at www.zelton-software.com. The company has two products: ZL Photo Manager and ZL Video Manager.

Customers can buy software on the website and pay by credit card. They can buy software on CD-ROM (Zelton sends the CD-ROMs to customers by mail), or they can download software from the website (but if they download, they can't copy the software to CD-ROM).

Now ask your partner these questions about Travel Ticket Central's website. Complete the answers.

... book flights at the website?	Yes/No
... buy train tickets?	Yes/No
... pay by credit card?	Yes/No
How ... receive tickets?	By ....
... download tickets + print?	Yes/No
... website address?	Website: ....

COMMUNICATION PRACTICE 13
(5.1, EXERCISE 4)

Student A

You need to have a meeting with some colleagues at a hotel in New York. Phone the Statesman Hotel and ask your partner for information about the business facilities.

- The meeting is for 12 people.
- You need 2 meeting rooms. Each room needs to have:
    - a table and chairs for 6 people
    - power sockets for laptops
    - an Internet connection (phone socket) – to send and receive emails.
- You need to make photocopies and send faxes.
- Ask what facilities there are for drinks and snacks.

COMMUNICATION PRACTICE 14
(5.2, EXERCISE 4)

Student A

You are a visitor at a company. You are at the reception desk. Ask your partner for directions to these rooms.

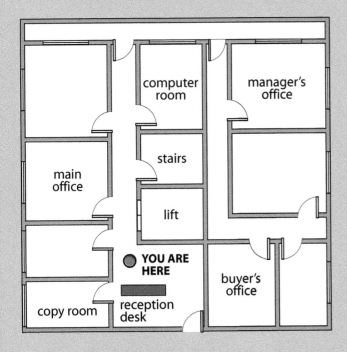

- the meeting room
- the mail room
- the interview room
- the call centre

Change roles. Answer your partner's questions. Give directions from the reception desk.

COMMUNICATION PRACTICE 15
(5.3, EXERCISE 5)

Student A

Imagine you live in the property below. Talk to your partner about your home.

- Toronto
- apartment
- 35th floor
- very modern
- 180m²
- 3 bedrooms

Now ask your partner about his/her home. Complete the information.

location: _____ km from _____
house/apartment
_____ bedrooms
_____ floors
garden: _____ m²
swimming pool: big/small

COMMUNICATION PRACTICE 16
(6.1, EXERCISE 4)

Take it in turns to ask and answer questions. Find out how often your partner does these things and fill in the chart.

	often	sometimes	not often	never
1 send emails	☐	☐	☐	☐
2 make international phone calls	☐	☐	☐	☐
3 go on business trips abroad	☐	☐	☐	☐
4 have meetings with foreign colleagues	☐	☐	☐	☐
5 give presentations	☐	☐	☐	☐
6 go to trade fairs	☐	☐	☐	☐
7 go to conferences	☐	☐	☐	☐

COMMUNICATION PRACTICE 17
(6.2, EXERCISE 3)

Student A

Phone your partner and ask to speak to these people. What are they doing? Make notes.

B   Hello.
A   Hello. Is ... there, ... ?
B   No, he's/she's ... .
A   Oh, right. OK. Thanks.

Anna: _____
Lia: _____
Pierre: _____
Nicole: _____

Now answer the phone and tell your partner what these people are doing.

George: work at home today
Karen: visit supplier's factory today
Frank: project in Japan
Helena: Hamburg office this week

COMMUNICATION PRACTICE 18
(6.3, EXERCISE 3)

What do you think these people do in their spare time? Choose three or four activities for each person. Imagine you are one of the people. Talk about your leisure activities – what you like/don't like. Your partner guesses which person you are. Change roles.

A I go/play/do … .
   I love/hate … .
B Are you Person 1/2/3/4?

COMMUNICATION PRACTICE 19
(7.1, EXERCISE 4)

Student A

Arrange to meet your partner next month. Arrange a date and time. You are busy on the highlighted dates.

Are you free/busy … ?
Can you make it … ?

M	T	W	T	F
1	2	3	4	5
8	9	10	11	12
15	16	17	18	19
22	23	24	25	26
29	30	31		

COMMUNICATION PRACTICE 20
(7.2, EXERCISE 3)

Student A

Imagine you are going on a business trip next week. Complete the information about your trip.

Destination: ------------------
Transport: ------------------
Departure date: ------------------
Departure time: ------------------
Arrival time: ------------------
Meeting with: ------------------
Return date: ------------------
Departure time: ------------------
Arrival time: ------------------

Your partner is also going on a business trip next week. Ask your partner questions about his/her trip and make notes.

Destination: ------------------
Transport: ------------------
Departure date: ------------------
Departure time: ------------------
Arrival time: ------------------
Meeting with: ------------------
Return date: ------------------
Departure time: ------------------
Arrival time: ------------------

Now answer your partner's questions about your business trip.

COMMUNICATION PRACTICE 21
(7.3, EXERCISE 3)

Student A

Your partner works at a ticket office. Use this information and buy a train ticket. Write down the fare.

1 Destination: London
2 Ticket: return
3 Leaving on: Wednesday (next week)
4 Leaving at: 08.10
5 Returning on: Thursday (next week)
6 Returning at: 16.55
7 Class: standard
8 Fare: £_____

Change roles. Your partner wants to buy a ticket.

1 Destination: ....
2 Ticket (single/return): ....
3 Leaving on (day): ....
4 Leaving at (time): ....
5 Returning on (day): ....
6 Returning at (time): ....
7 Class (first/standard): ....
8 Fare: £34.50

COMMUNICATION PRACTICE 22
(8.1, EXERCISE 3a)

Student A

Last week, your partner was on a training course. Ask questions about it. Complete the information.

Course (name): ....
Good? ....
Location: ....
Number of people: ....
Trainer (name): ....

Last week, you were at a conference. Answer your partner's questions about it. Use this information.

International Finance Conference
In Zurich
600 people
Key speaker: Professor Werner Schmidt
Very good

COMMUNICATION PRACTICE 23
(8.2, EXERCISE 3)

Student A

You are your partner's manager. Last week, he/she visited a customer in Liverpool. Ask questions about the business trip. Make notes.

... Good trip? ....
What company ... visit? ....
How ... travel? ....
Where ... stay? ....
Who ... talk to? ....
... discuss ... new products? ....
... customer ... like the products? ....

Now your partner is your manager. Last week, you visited a supplier's factory in Stuttgart. Answer your manager's questions about the business trip. Use this information.

Trip: good
Company: Klettbeton AG
Travel: by plane
Hotel: Hotel Alpenblick / city centre
Factory: very modern, with new warehouse
Talked to: Dieter Mann (Sales Manager) Karl Springer (Production Manager)
Discussed: factory and production process

COMMUNICATION PRACTICE 24
(8.3, EXERCISE 4)

Student A

Last month, your partner went on holiday. Ask him/her as many questions as you can about it.

Where ...?   When ...?   How ...?   What ...?
Did you ...?   Was/Were ...?

Last month, you went on holiday. Answer your partner's questions. Use this information.

Destination: New Zealand, South Island
Transport: flight
Departure: 9th (last month)
Return: 28th (last month)
Accommodation: camping – rented a car, travelled
Activities: sightseeing, walking, swimming
Good holiday? very good

COMMUNICATION PRACTICE 25
(9.1, EXERCISE 3)

It's Monday morning. Five minutes ago, you received this email from a colleague.

> Dear .... ,
> Are we having a team meeting this week? If we are, do you know when and where? Also, I don't have the minutes of the last meeting.
> Regards,
> Nicola

In pairs, write a reply. Use this information.

- Say you are sorry she didn't receive the information.
- Meeting next Tuesday afternoon / 2 pm / your office.
- Ask her to phone or send an email if there is a problem.
- Attach: minutes (meeting last week) / agenda (meeting this week).

Exchange your email with another pair of students. Write a reply to their email and ask them a question. Exchange replies.

COMMUNICATION PRACTICE 26
(9.2, EXERCISE 4)

Student A

You are Sam/Samantha Gray from Imporex. Your phone number is 05675 2900928.

Make this phone call:

Telephone Everest Consulting. Ask to speak to Tony Davey. If he isn't in the office, ask if he can call you back.

Sit back-to-back with your partner. Start the call.

Now, you are John/Jane Spencer. You work for Connex. Answer the phone when your partner calls you.

Answer the phone.
↓
Betty Colley's line is busy.
↓
Ask if the caller would like to hold.
↓
Take a message (name, company, number).
↓
Thank the caller and say goodbye.

COMMUNICATION PRACTICE 27
(9.3, EXERCISE 3)

You and your partner each choose a city (1–10). Ask questions about the weather to work out which city your partner is in. Take it in turns to choose another city.

A What's the weather like?
B It's ... .
A Is it very/quite hot/cold?
B Yes. / No. It's very/quite ... .
A Are you in ...?

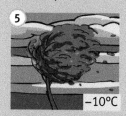
Santiago, Chile — 12°C

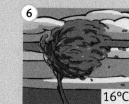
Paris, France — 6°C

London, UK — 4°C

Beijing, China — −8°C

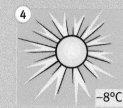
Berlin, Germany — −10°C

Los Angeles, USA — 16°C

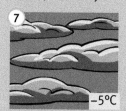
Montreal, Canada — −5°C

Helsinki, Finland — −12°C

Auckland, New Zealand — 20°C

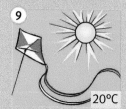
Jakarta, Indonesia — 28°C

COMMUNICATION PRACTICE 28
(10.1, EXERCISE 4)

Work with a partner. Make comparisons and discuss the advantages and disadvantages of each type of transport. Decide with your partner the best way to travel in the situations.

… is more/less … than … .
One advantage/disadvantage is … .

a for company executive travel

private jet

private helicopter

b for travel in a city

motorbike

bike

c for a journey to work

underground   car

COMMUNICATION PRACTICE 29
(10.2, EXERCISE 3)

You and your partner both work for a company in Paris. Next month, you're going on a business trip to Frankfurt. Use this information to find the best way to travel. Find a compromise between speed, cost and convenience.

I think … .
Yes, I agree. / Yes, that's true.
I'm not sure.
I prefer … .
What do you think?

Trip: Paris → Frankfurt

transport	return fare	journey time
Plane (1)	€640 per person	1h 15 (direct)
Plane (2)	€260 per person	3h 30 (one stop)
Train	€160 per person	6h 30 (direct)
Car	€850 for one car	6h 00

Notes: Journey times by plane are airport-to-airport, and by train, station-to-station.

Costs for car travel include fuel and motorway tolls.

COMMUNICATION PRACTICE 30
(10.3, EXERCISE 3)

Student A

You are an assistant at an airline check-in desk. Your partner is a passenger who wants to check in. Have a conversation. Use this information to ask and answer questions.

- ID?
- Seat position?
- Luggage?
- Give the passenger his/her boarding pass.
- Gate B7.
- Departure = 15 mins late.

Now you are a passenger. Check in for your flight. You have a small briefcase and a large suitcase. Ask if the flight is on time.

COMMUNICATION PRACTICE 31
(11.1, EXERCISE 3)

Next month, some British colleagues are coming to your company (in your home town) for a meeting. They're arriving at 5.00 pm on the 15th and they're leaving after the meeting on the 16th.

Conversation 1

Make plans for the meeting. Discuss these points with your partner.

What/Where shall we …?   Shall we …?   Let's… .

- Which hotel?
- Dinner on 15th – where?
- Lunch on 16th – where?

Conversation 2

Now look at the list of the arrangements you need to make. What are the most urgent jobs? Discuss with your partner and put them in order.

First, … . Then, … . Before/After that, … . Finally, … .

- [ ] Book the restaurant.
- [ ] Book the hotel.
- [ ] Check how many are coming.
- [ ] Arrange transport to and from the airport.
- [ ] Send a schedule of the trip to colleagues.

COMMUNICATION PRACTICE 32
(11.2, EXERCISE 5)

You work for a large international company. Next year, your company wants to hold a conference for some of its managers. You and your partner have to organise the conference.

Talk about this list of jobs you have to do. Put them in order, from most to least urgent.

- [ ] Make a list of people we're going to invite.
- [ ] Arrange the timing: number of days, dates.
- [ ] Choose a location: country and city.
- [ ] Choose accommodation: hotel? conference centre?
- [ ] Plan the events at the conference: presentations, meetings …
- [ ] Send invitations.
- [ ] Write a brochure giving information about the conference.

Now tell another pair of students about your plans. Explain the reasons for the order of your plans.

First / Then / After that … .
We're going to … because … .
Our aim/objective is to … .

COMMUNICATION PRACTICE 33
(11.3, EXERCISE 3)

Student A

Your name is Mr/Ms Garner. You're going to stay at the Elm Hotel. Your partner is the receptionist. Check in – say you've got a reservation, and then answer the receptionist's questions. Use this information.

Type of room:	👤👤
Nights:	3

You need to get up early in the morning – at 6.30.

Now you're the receptionist. Your partner is going to check out. Use this information.

Room number:	133
Type of room:	👤
Nights:	2

€130 per night x 2 nights = **€260**

Extras:

Phone calls: 1	€8
Minibar: 1 mineral water	€2
Total extras	**€10**

Total bill: €260 + €10 = €270

Notes: Guest's company, ITS, paying bill. Guest paying extras.

COMMUNICATION PRACTICE 34
(12.1, EXERCISE 4)

Student A

Look at your company's results for the last two quarters. Talk to your partner. Describe how well/ badly business is doing. Say if things are improving, and how quickly.

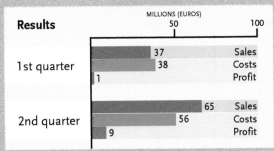

Results	MILLIONS (EUROS) 50	100	
1st quarter	37		Sales
	38		Costs
	1		Profit
2nd quarter	65		Sales
	56		Costs
	9		Profit

Now ask your partner how business is. Show you're interested in what he/she says.

COMMUNICATION PRACTICE 35
(12.2, EXERCISE 3)

Student A

You and your partner work for Toreador Sports. You are buyers. Use the information to answer your partner's questions about the product from Montego Accessories. Then, ask your partner about the product from Tempora, and complete the information.

How much/many ...?

Toreador Sports – **Product File**

Supplier: Montego Accessories

Product: 'Mistral' baseball cap

Product cost (full price): €10.00

Number of products in stock: 5,000

Discount: 10%

Price in store: $16.00

Products sold last week: 3,260 products

Profit from last week: $40,685

Toreador Sports – **Product File**

Supplier: Tempora

Product: 'Challenger' watch

Product cost (full price): €.........................

Number of products in stock: ....

Discount: ....%

Price in store: $.........................

Products sold last week: .... products

Profit from last week: $.........................

COMMUNICATION PRACTICE 36
(12.3, EXERCISE 3)

Take it in turns to role play a customer and a shop assistant. The customer wants to look at and buy the things in the photos.

How much ...?   Could I ...?   Can I pay by ...?
Of course.   Sure.   No problem.   I'll go and get ... .

€10,000

€79

€15

€85

COMMUNICATION PRACTICE 4
(2.1, EXERCISE 5)

Student B

Exchange numbers with Student A. Write the numbers.

A What's your ... number?
B It's ... .
A Sorry?
B It's ... .
A So, ...
B That's right.

Student B		Student A	
Tel:	1883 03456680	Tel:	....
Mobile:	0545223090	Mobile:	....
Fax:	1883 05339178	Fax:	....
email:	j_carr@gpv.com	email:	....

COMMUNICATION PRACTICE 7
(3.1, EXERCISE 3)

Student B

Ask and answer questions. Fill in the chart. Student B starts.

Where ... live?   What ... do?   What company ... work for?   Where ... work?   How do you spell that?

	Home	Job	Company	Place
1				
2	Madrid	accountant	Top Media	office
3				
4	London	shop assistant	Maxis Home	sales shop
5				
6	Milan	engineer	Electrina	factory

COMMUNICATION PRACTICE 8
(3.2, EXERCISE 6)

Student B

Ask and answer questions. Fill in the chart.

Where ... come from / live?   What company ... own?

Name	Comes from	Lives	Company
Ana Pons	Barcelona		Practical PLC
Hans Bauer			Teknix
Sandy Cohen	New York		Novalink
Michael Pitt		San Francisco	
Claire Garnier	Montpellier		TM Mode
Pedro Cruz		Prague	

COMMUNICATION PRACTICE 10
(4.1, EXERCISE 4)

Student B

Read this page from a report about business on the Internet. Ask your partner questions. Find out what the words in highlight stand for/mean and complete the notes. Answer your partner's questions.

... mean?   ... stand for?   ... spell ...?   ... say that again?   ... speak slowly?

Business on the Internet – Contents

Page

3 Business online = *on the Internet*

7 What is 'e-business'? = ...

11 A name for your URL = *Uniform Resource Locator* = *a website address*

13 B2B = ...
– business connections

17 The webmaster = *a website manager*

20 Buy the right PC = ...

COMMUNICATION PRACTICE 11
(4.2, EXERCISE 4)

Student B

Write an email to your partner (on paper). Ask for the address of his/her office.

Your partner will send you an email. Write a reply.

COMMUNICATION PRACTICE 12
(4.3, EXERCISE 4)

Student B

Ask your partner these questions about Zelton Software's website. Complete the answers.

... buy software from the website?	Yes/No
What software ... buy?	Software: _____
... pay by credit card?	Yes/No
... download software?	Yes/No
... copy software/CD?	Yes/No
... buy software/CD?	Yes/No
... website address?	Website: _____

Now read about Travel Ticket Central's website, then answer your partner's questions.

At Travel Ticket Central's website (www.travel-ticket-central.com) customers can buy plane tickets (but not train tickets). Customers pay by credit card on the website. Travel Ticket Central sends customers their tickets by mail (customers can't download and print tickets).

COMMUNICATION PRACTICE 13
(5.1, EXERCISE 4)

Student B

You work at the Statesman Hotel in New York. Student A phones to ask about your business facilities. Use this information to answer the questions:

Facilities in the hotel business centre:

6 meeting rooms:

3 rooms for 4–6 people

2 rooms for 10–12 people

1 room for 15–20 people

Facilities in the meeting rooms:

chairs and tables

power sockets (no phone sockets)

Facilities in reception:

a photocopier

a fax machine

a computer with Internet connection

a drinks machine

There's a bar and restaurant at the hotel.

COMMUNICATION PRACTICE 14
(5.2, EXERCISE 4)

Student B

You are at the reception desk of your company. Your partner is a visitor. Answer your partner's questions. Give directions from the reception desk.

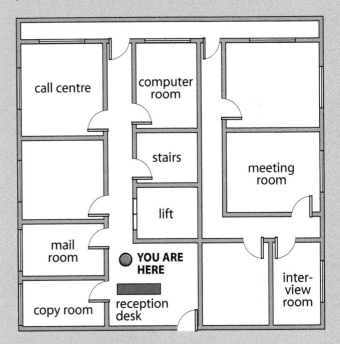

Change roles. Ask your partner for directions to these rooms:

- the buyer's office
- the copy room
- the main office
- the manager's office

COMMUNICATION PRACTICE 15
(5.3, EXERCISE 5)

Student B

Ask your partner about his/her home. Complete the information.

city: ....

house/apartment

.... floor

quite/very old/modern

............m²

.... bedroom(s)

Now imagine you live in the property below. Talk to your partner about your home.

- 30 km from Madrid
- 6 bedrooms
- small swimming pool
- house
- 3 floors
- garden: 3,500 m²

COMMUNICATION PRACTICE 17
(6.2, EXERCISE 3)

Student B

Answer the phone and tell your partner what these people are doing.

B   Hello.
A   Hello. Is ... there, ... ?
B   No, he's/she's ... .
A   Oh, right. OK. Thanks.

Anna: lunch at the moment
Lia: meeting this morning
Pierre: off this week
Nicole: project abroad

Phone your partner and ask to speak to these people. What are they doing? Make notes.

George: ....
Karen: ....
Frank: ....
Helena: ....

COMMUNICATION PRACTICE 19
(7.1, EXERCISE 4)

Student B

Arrange to meet your partner next month. Arrange a date and time. You are busy on the highlighted dates.

Are you free/busy ... ?
Can you make it ... ?

M	T	W	T	F
1	2	3	4	5
8	9	10	11	12
15	16	17	18	19
22	23	24	25	26
29	30	31		

COMMUNICATION PRACTICE 20
(7.2, EXERCISE 3)

Student B

Imagine you are going on a business trip next week. Complete the information about your trip.

Destination: ....
Transport: ....
Departure date: ....
Departure time: ....
Arrival time: ....
Meeting with: ....
Return date: ....
Departure time: ....
Arrival time: ....

Now answer your partner's questions about your business trip.

Your partner is also going on a business trip next week. Ask your partner questions about his/her trip and make notes.

Destination: ....
Transport: ....
Departure date: ....
Departure time: ....
Arrival time: ....
Meeting with: ....
Return date: ....
Departure time: ....
Arrival time: ....

COMMUNICATION PRACTICE 21
(7.3, EXERCISE 3)

Student B

You work at a ticket office. Your partner wants to buy a train ticket. Complete the information.

1 Destination: ....
2 Ticket (single/return): ....
3 Leaving on (day): ....
4 Leaving at (time): ....
5 Returning on (day): ....
6 Returning at (time): ....
7 Class (first/standard): ....
8 Fare: £19.60

Change roles. Use this information and buy a ticket from your partner. Write down the fare.

1 Destination: Cambridge
2 Ticket: return
3 Leaving on: Monday (next week)
4 Leaving at: 07.45
5 Returning on: Monday (next week)
6 Returning at: 18.20
7 Class: standard
8 Fare: £....................

COMMUNICATION PRACTICE 22
(8.1, EXERCISE 3a)

Student B

Last week, you were on a training course. Answer your partner's questions about it. Use this information.

Course: Making Presentations
Head office
26 people
Trainer: Rita Davies – sales manager
Quite good, but very long

Last week, your partner was at a conference. Ask questions about it. Complete the information.

Conference (name): ....
Good? ....
Location: ....
Number of people: ....
Key speaker (name): ....

COMMUNICATION PRACTICE 23
(8.2, EXERCISE 3)

Student B

Last week, you visited a customer in Liverpool. Your partner is your manager. Answer his/her questions about the visit. Use this information.

Trip: very good
Company: Stone and Sons
Travel: by train
Hotel: small hotel near customer's office
Talked to: Tom Fellows (manager) and Jane Lark (buyer)
Discussed: you presented your new products
Customer's opinion: liked products

Now you are your partner's manager. Last week, he/she visited a supplier's factory in Stuttgart. Ask questions about the business trip. Make notes.

... good trip? ....
What company ... visit? ....
How ... travel? ....
Where ... stay? ....
... factory good? ....
Who ... talk to? ....
What ... talk about? ....

COMMUNICATION PRACTICE 24
(8.3, EXERCISE 4)

Student B

Last month, you went on holiday. Answer your partner's questions. Use this information.

Destination: Bermuda – package tour
Transport: flight
Departure: 5th (last month)
Return: 21st (last month)
Accommodation: hotel 100 metres from beach
Activities: swimming, golf, sightseeing (rented a car)
Good holiday? very good

Last month, your partner went on holiday. Ask him/her as many questions as you can about it.

Where ...?   When ...?   How ...?   What ...?
Did you ...?   Was/Were ...?

COMMUNICATION PRACTICE 26
(9.2, EXERCISE 4)

Student B

You are Chris/Christina Black. You work for Everest Consulting. Sit back to back with your partner. Answer the phone when he/she calls you.

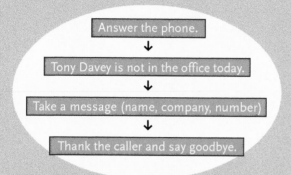

Answer the phone.
↓
Tony Davey is not in the office today.
↓
Take a message (name, company, number)
↓
Thank the caller and say goodbye.

Now, you are Carl/Carla Willan from Pantek. Your phone number is 18789 10338799.

Make this phone call:

Telephone Connex. Ask to speak to Betty Colley. If she isn't in the office, or the line is busy, ask if she can call you back.

Start the call.

COMMUNICATION PRACTICE 30
(10.3, EXERCISE 3)

Student B

You are a passenger. Your partner is an assistant at an airline check-in desk. Check in for your flight. You have one large bag with you. Ask if the flight is on time.

Now you are an assistant at the check-in desk. Your partner is a passenger who wants to check in. Have a conversation. Use this information to ask and answer questions.

- ID?
- Seat position?
- Luggage?
- Give the passenger his/her boarding pass.
- Gate C12.
- No delays.

COMMUNICATION PRACTICE 33
(11.3, EXERCISE 3)

Student B

You're a receptionist at the Elm Hotel. Your partner is a guest who is going to check in. Use the information on the reservations card.

Reservations:	G			
Last name:	Garner	Gardner	Gaston	Geiger
Type of room:	👤👤	👤	👤	👤👤
Nights:	2	3	1	2
Room number:	423	109	325	158

Information/Questions for guests
Breakfast: 7.00 – 9.00
Wake-up call?

Now you are a guest at the Elm Hotel. You are checking out. Your company (ITS) is paying the bill. You have to pay the extras.

Room number:	133
Type of room:	👤
Nights:	2

Extras: one phone call + a mineral water from the minibar.

COMMUNICATION PRACTICE 34
(12.1, EXERCISE 4)

Student B

Ask your partner how business is. Show you're interested in what he/she says.

Now look at the results for your company for the last two quarters. Describe how well/badly business is doing. Say if things are improving, and how quickly.

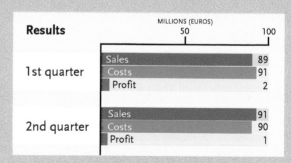

Results	MILLIONS (EUROS) 50	100
1st quarter	Sales	89
	Costs	91
	Profit	2
2nd quarter	Sales	91
	Costs	90
	Profit	1

Student B

You and your partner work for Toreador Sports. You are buyers. Ask your partner about the product from Montego Accessories and complete the information. Then, use the information to answer your partner's questions about the product from Tempora.

How much/many ...?

Toreador Sports – **Product File**

Supplier: Montego Accessories
Product: 'Mistral' baseball cap

Product cost (full price): €......................
Number of products in stock: ....
Discount: ....%
Price in store: $......................
Products sold last week: .... products
Profit from last week: $......................

Toreador Sports – **Product File**

Supplier: Tempora
Product: 'Challenger' watch

Product cost (full price): €48.00
Number of products in stock: 300
Discount: 15%
Price in store: $60.00
Products sold last week: 75 products
Profit from last week: $2,115

Grammar and vocabulary practice

1 Fill in the missing letters to complete the conversation.

Paul ¹_H_i. I'm Paul Canning.

Kate ²H _ l _ _ Paul. I'm Kate Brown.

Paul ³_ _ _ e to meet you. ⁴_ _ l _ _ m _ to Chicago.

Kate ⁵_ _ _ nk _ .

2 Fill in the gaps with the correct form of *be*.

1 I'm Paul Reed and this is Julia Bell. _We're_ from Zap Productions.

2 This is Diana Edison. _____ from CCC.

3 This is Alan Parker and this is Alan Dale. _____ from NorthNet.

4 This is George Carter. _____ from B-Line.

5 I'm David Clark. _____ from Safeguard.

3 Put the words in order. Make questions and answers.

1 she / from / where's ?
   Where's she from?
   Beijing / from / she's .
   _____

2 from / Jim / London / is ?
   _____
   Manchester / from / no / he's .
   _____

3 from / they / are / where ?
   _____
   Montpellier / in / from / France / they're .
   _____

4 are / where / from / you ?
   _____
   Badajoz / in / I'm / from / Spain .
   _____

5 you / Germany / are / from ?
   _____
   from / I'm / no / Austria .
   _____

4 Fill in the gaps.

1 Marseille is in the s_outh_ of F_____ .

2 Gdansk is in the n_____ of P_____ .

3 Birmingham is in the c_____ of the U_____ .

4 Valencia is in the e_____ of S_____ .

5 Bonn is in the w_____ of G_____ .

5 Fill in the gaps with *a* or *an*.

1 Would you like _a_ coffee?

2 Could I have ____ mineral water, please?

3 ____ iced tea, please.

4 A Would you like a drink?
   B Yes, ____ orange juice, please.

5 Would you like ____ tea?

6 Could I have ____ drink, please?

6 Put the conversation in order. Write 1–5 in the boxes.

a [ ] Sugar, please. No milk.

b [ ] Yes. Would you like milk and sugar?

c [ ] OK. A coffee with sugar.

d [1] Would you like a drink?

e [ ] Yes, please. Could I have a coffee?

1 This is your business card. Fill in the gaps.

1 My _telephone number_ is 0208 8062345.

2 My _____ is 17, Church Road.

3 My _____ is 07762148411.

4 My _____ is 0208 8062757.

5 My _____ is dkp@yt-line.com

Dan Powers
Marketing Consultant

17 Church Road, London N89 9BT

Tel: 0208 8062345   Mobile: 07762148411

Fax: 0208 8062757   email: dkp@yt-line.com

2 Put the words in order. Make sentences.

1 telephone / what's / number / your ?
   What's your telephone number?

2 what's / address / your / email ?
   ----

3 the / fax / what's / number ?
   ----

4 mobile / your / what's / phone / number ?
   ----

5 email / this / address / my / is .
   ----

3 Write the numbers.

1 fourteen *14*   5 forty-seven _____
2 thirty _____   6 eleven _____
3 twenty-one _____   7 fifty _____
4 fifty-one _____   8 thirty-nine _____

4 Write the times as words.

1 11.20
   twenty past eleven

2 5.15
   ----

3 8.30
   ----

4 12.40
   ----

5 7.05
   ----

6 3.45
   ----

7 12.00
   ----

8 9.25
   ----

9 11.35
   ----

10 12.50
   ----

5 Fill in the gaps.

at   what   when's   it's   what's   excuse

1 *Excuse* me. _____ time is it?
2 A _____ the time?
   B _____ half past two.
3 _____ the next train to Brussels?
4 The next train is _____ three o'clock.

6 Match the numbers to the words.

1 100   a sixty-two
2 70   b a hundred
3 62   c seventy
4 80   d eighty-nine
5 94   e ninety-one
6 73   f ninety-four
7 89   g eighty
8 91   h seventy-three

7 Write the plurals for these words.

1 snack   *snacks*
2 drink   --------------
3 dollar   --------------
4 euro   --------------
5 city   --------------
6 fax   --------------
7 student   --------------
8 company   --------------
9 phone number   --------------
10 email address --------------

UNIT 3

1 Fill in the missing letters to make jobs and workplaces.

1 I'm an a *ccountan*t. I work in an
   o _ _ _ _ e.
2 He's an e _ _ _ _ _ _ r. He works in a
   f _ _ _ _ _ y.
3 She's a t _ _ _ n _ _ _ _ n. She works in a
   l _ b.
4 I'm a s _ _ _ s a _ _ _ _ _ _ _ t. I work in
   a s _ _ p.
5 She's a r _ _ _ _ _ _ _ n _ _ t. She works in
   a h _ _ _ l.

2 Make questions for these answers.

1 *Where do you live?* ------------------------------
   Dublin.

2 -- ?
   ICT Chemicals.

3 -- ?
   In the head office, in Dublin.

4 -- ?
   I'm a sales manager.

3 Fill in the gaps.

have buy sell make own come from

1 Southland companies ___sell___ products for the office.
2 350 million customers _____ their products each year.
3 James and Ross Milburn _____ the Southland Group.
4 James and Ross Milburn _____ the USA.
5 They _____ 32 factories.
6 They _____ 48 different products in their factories.

4 Write the numbers as words.

1 735   *seven hundred and thirty-five*
2 400   _____
3 6,900   _____
4 35,000   _____
5 7.5   _____
6 2,000,000 _____
7 8.2 billion _____
8 50,000,000 _____

5 Write the correct form of the verb.

1 David Thomas ___owns___ a small company. (to own)
2 They _____ products for the home. (to sell)
3 I _____ from suppliers in Germany. (to buy)
4 We _____ two factories in France. (to have)
5 Sarah Taylor _____ Chicago. (to come from)
6 The factories _____ mobile phones. (to make)

6 Fill in the gaps in the questions with *do* or *does*.

1 Where ___does___ Eva Bianchi live?
  She lives in Rome.
2 _____ James Bernard own 50% of Orion?
  Yes, he owns 50%.
3 Where _____ Goran Tatić come from?
  He comes from Croatia.
4 _____ Southland factories make office products?
  Yes, they make office products.
5 _____ you sell products on the Internet?
  Yes, we sell products on the Internet.

7 Make seven sentences.

I She He They	finish start have get	breakfast work lunch up a break dinner	at	5.30 pm 7.15 am 9.00 am 12.15 pm 7.00 am 11.00 am 8.00 am

1 *I get up at 7.00 am.* _____ 2

  She has breakfast at 7.15 am.

3 _____
4 _____
5 _____
6 _____

8 Make negative sentences.

1 My company has a cafeteria.
  My company doesn't have a cafeteria.
2 Alan is in the office.
  _____
3 I have the phone number.
  _____
4 Sharon works in the Melbourne office
  _____
5 We sell the product.
  _____
6 I'm an engineer.
  _____

UNIT 4

1 Fill in the gaps.

know mean understand spell stand sure

1 How do you ___spell___ 'information'?
2 A What does this _____ ?
  B I don't _____ .
3 A I think 'B2B' means 'business-to-business'.
  B Are you _____ ?
4 A What does UPS _____ for?
  B United Parcel Service.
5 A Do you _____ this email in English?
  B Yes.

2 Put the words in order. Make sentences.

1 you / could / that / say / again ?
Could you say that again?

2 spell / you / that / could ?
_____

3 could / slowly / more / speak / you ?
_____

4 repeat / your / you / could / please / name ?
_____

5 me / write / could / for / number / the / you ?
_____

3 Fill in the gaps in the email.

dear   manager   message   Mr   regards
send   thank

```
 ┌──────────────────────────┐
 │  ⬭⬭⬭                      │
 ├──────────────────────────┤
 │  To: Nick Planter         │
 │  ¹ Dear  ² _____ Planter,│
 │                           │
 │  ³ _____ you for your ⁴ _____ .│
 │  Could you ⁵ _____ your telephone│
 │  number?                  │
 │  Best ⁶ _____ ,          │
 │  Ed Fisher                │
 │  Human Resources ⁷ _____ │
 └──────────────────────────┘
```

4 Fill in the gaps.

my   's   your   his   of   her   our   their

1 John and Rita are in ___*their*___ office.
2 Mr Evans is the sales manager. This is _____ phone number.
3 I have Ms Wade's email address, but I don't have _____ fax number.
4 We make the products at _____ factory in China.
5 I have a mobile phone. _____ number is 0589 198273801.
6 A Do you have a fax?
   B Yes.
   A What's _____ fax number?
7 What's the number _____ the Paris office?
8 What's Jan _____ email address?

5 Fill in gaps in the computer expressions.

software   print   save   copy   files (x2)
music

computer < *software*
          _____

_____
_____ > a document
_____

download < _____

6 Put the words in order. Make sentences.

1 buy / products / where / I / can / the ?
Where can I buy the products?

2 CDs / I / how / the / can / copy ?
_____

3 the / can't / read / I / file .
_____

4 your / have / email / can / address / I ?
_____

5 website / this / you / download / can't / from / music .
_____

6 Internet / on / buy / can / books / where / we / the ?
_____

UNIT 5

1 Fill in the missing letters to complete the sentences.

1 You can use our f <u>a</u> x m _ _ _ _ _ e to send a message.
2 You can use the hotel p _ _ _ _ c _ _ _ _ r to make copies.
3 We can't plug in the laptop because there are no p _ _ _ r s _ _ _ _ s.
4 Each computer in the room has a p _ _ _ _ _ r.
5 Can you book a m _ _ _ _ _ g r _ _ m for tomorrow at 10 am?
6 I can draw a diagram on the f _ _ p c _ _ _ t.

Fill in the gaps with the correct form of *there is / are*.

1 ? _____Is there_____ a drinks machine here?
2 ✓ _____ a photocopier in the office.
3 ✓ _____ two messages for you.
4 ✗ _____ a fax machine here.
5 ? _____ two power sockets in the room?
6 ? _____ a phone I can use?
7 ✓ _____ 20 stores in this country.
8 ✗ _____ two managers at the factory.

Make sentences.

1 I / need / use / photocopier .
   I need to use a photocopier.

2 she / need / phone / the office .
   _____

3 I / need / new computer .
   _____

4 he / need / mobile phone .
   _____

5 they / need / meet / the customer .
   _____

Write the ordinal numbers as words.

1 His office is on the _____*fifth*_____ (5th) floor.
2 The lift is at the _____ (10th) floor.
3 Reception is on the _____ (1st) floor.
4 The Zantek offices are on the _____-_____ (22nd) and _____-_____ (28th) floors.
5 There's a very good view from my office on the _____-_____ (33rd) floor.
6 There are meeting rooms on the _____ (7th) floor.

Fill in the gaps.

turn	where's	on	over	through	where
end	excuse	past	please		

1 A _____*Excuse*_____ me.
  B Yes?
  A _____ the lift, please?
  B The lift? It's _____ there, just _____ the stairs.

2 A _____ are the toilets, _____ ?
  B Go to the _____ of the corridor and _____ right.
  A _____ the doors?
  B Yes, and it's the second door _____ your left.

Make sentences using imperatives.

right	past the lift	to the end of the corridor
left	through the doors	

1 _____*Turn left.*_____
  _____

2 _____
  _____

3 _____
  _____

4 _____
  _____

5 _____
  _____

Homes. Fill in the missing letters.

1 I live in a two-room a͟ p͟a͟r͟t͟m͟e͟n͟t͟.
2 His h͟ _ _ _ e͟ is in the city centre.
3 We have TVs in the k͟ _ _ _ _ _ n͟ and in the l͟ _ _ _ _ g room.
4 The property is big. It has five b͟ _ _ _ _ _ _ s͟ and two b͟ _ _ h͟ _ _ _ _ s͟.
5 There's a swimming pool in the g͟ _ _ _ _ n͟.

8

Write the opposites of the adjectives.

1 hot _____*cold*_____
2 new _____
3 nice _____
4 cheap _____
5 high _____
6 small _____

9 Make sentences. Use *very* or *quite* and the adjectives.

1 The house has nine bedrooms and three bathrooms. *(big)*
The house is very big.

2 The building has six floors. *(high)*

3 My apartment has one bedroom and a living room. *(small)*

4 My kitchen is 40 m². *(large)*

5 The corridor is 7 m. *(long)*

UNIT 6

1 Fill in the gaps.

> conference   trips   meetings   fairs
> presentations

1 Do you go on business ___*trips*___ ?
2 I sometimes go to trade _____ .
3 I usually have _____ in my office.
4 I sometimes give _____ to large groups.
5 I go to our company _____ every year.

2 Add the words in brackets to the sentences.

1 I get up at 6.30. *(usually)*
I usually get up at 6.30.

2 I take work home. *(never)*

3 I don't send faxes. *(often)*

4 Do you go to trade fairs? *(sometimes)*

5 I have lunch at home. *(always)*

6 I go to meetings. *(a lot of)*

7 I don't go to conferences *(a lot)*

3 Fill in the missing letters to make 'present time' words.

1 What are you doing at the m <u>o m e</u> t?
2 We're working in the office n _ _.
3 Are they having the conference t _ _ _ week?
4 I'm working at home t _ _ _ _.

4 Make sentences. Use the present continuous.

1 he / have / coffee at the moment .
He's having coffee at the moment.

2 she / not / work / at home today .

3 you / leave / now ?

4 where / you / go ?

5 I / not / read / the report now .

6 what / you / do ?

7 he / have / lunch at the moment ?

8 they / not / have / a meeting this morning .

5 Underline the correct form of the verbs.

1 I love *swim/swimming*. I go every morning.
2 I like *watch/watching* football, but I can't *play/playing* very well.
3 I hate *run/running*. I much prefer *cycle/cycling*.
4 What do you like *do/doing* in your spare time?
5 I can't *ski/skiing* very well. It's very difficult.
6 I don't like *play/playing* chess. It's boring.

6 Fill in the gaps with correct form of *go*, *play* or *do*.

1 I ___*go*___ running.
2 Do you _____ football?
3 He _____ weight training.
4 She _____ aerobics after work.
5 I _____ cycling in the morning.
6 He _____ the guitar in a band.
7 They _____ fishing.

1 Write the dates as words.

1 10.05 _May the tenth_ / _the tenth of May_
2 14.07 _____ / _____
3 03.12 _____ / _____
4 05.11 _____ / _____
5 01.04 _____ / _____
6 22.01 _____ / _____

2 Fill in the gaps with *in*, *on*, or *at*.

1 I can make it _on_ the fifteenth.
2 Can we meet _____ the beginning of the month?
3 I'm going to the Toronto office the last week _____ March.
4 Our next meeting is _____ the end of April.
5 Vickie can see you _____ Thursday.
6 What about a meeting _____ the nineteenth?
7 I can phone you _____ the afternoon.
8 The presentation is _____ three o'clock.

3 Fill in the gaps.

busy   meet   free   make   fine   about

1 When can we _meet_ ?
2 When are you _____ ?
3 What _____ the fifth of June?
4 Yes, I can _____ it on the tenth of April.
5 No, I'm _____ on the thirtieth.
6 Ten o'clock? Yes, that's _____ .

4 Fill in the gaps.

driving   arriving   changing   flying coming   staying

1 A Where are you _staying_ in Avignon?
   B At the hotel Ibis.
2 A Are you _____ to Barcelona?
   B Yes, with Lufthansa.
3 A When are you _____ in London?
   B At 20.30.
4 A When are you _____ back from Zurich?
   B On Monday evening.
5 I'm _____ to Bologna this time. It's only two hours by car.
6 A Are you flying direct to Hong Kong?
   B No, I'm _____ in Amsterdam.

5 These are your arrangements for next week. Describe what you are doing.

| **Mon 1** |
| Fly to Frankfurt LH208 – 8.20 |
| Meeting: 2.30 Hans Baumann |
| **Tues 2** |
| Train > Cologne 8.00. |
| Dinner with Tony at hotel |
| **Wed 3** |
| Cologne office |
| **Thu 4** |
| Train to Frankfurt 1.30 |
| Fly home LH209 – 5.35 |
| **Fri 5** |
| Give presentation – 2.30 |
| Finish early (drink with Jill) |
| **Sat 6** |
| Golf – 9.30 |
| **Sun 7** |

1 _On Monday morning, I'm flying to Frankfurt._
2 _____
3 _____
4 _____
5 _____
6 _____

6 Buying a train ticket. Fill in the gaps.

1 A s_ingle_ or a return ticket?
2 I don't know the times of trains. Do you have a t_____ ?
3 What time does the train a_____ in London?
4 Can I r_____ a seat, please?
5 A first or second c_____ ticket?
6 How much is the f_____ from London to Paris?

7 Complete the questions to match the answers.

1 A _Where_ would you like to go?

B I'd like to go to Milan.

2 A _____ do you want to pay?

B I want to pay by credit card.

3 A _____ you like a single or a return?

B I'd like a single, please.

4 A _____ do you want to come back?

B I want to come back on Monday.

5 A _____ you like to book a seat now?

B Yes, I'd like to book a seat now.

6 A _____ you want to travel second class?

B No, I want to travel first class, please.

UNIT 8

1 Fill in the gaps with *was*, *wasn't*, *were* or *weren't*.

1 A Where _were_ you yesterday?

B We _____ in a meeting.

2 A _____ you at the conference in Paris last month?

B Yes, I _____ in Paris.

3 A _____ Julia at the trade fair last year?

B No, she _____ there.

4 A _____ they at the presentation yesterday?

B No, they _____ there. They _____ on a trip.

2 Fill in the gaps.

yesterday weeks ago morning last night

1 He was in New York ten days _____ .

2 Today is Monday so, _____ was Sunday.

3 I was in Australia _____ month.

4 The trade fair was three _____ ago.

5 They were in the office this _____ .

6 There was a problem at the factory last _____ .

3 Match the pairs to make sentences. Write a–e in the boxes.

1 [c] She presented

2 [ ] We didn't talk

3 [ ] They discussed

4 [ ] I visited the factory

5 [ ] We didn't look

a at the new office.

b about work over lunch.

c the new project at the presentation.

d prices at the meeting

e to see the new production line.

4 Make sentences in the past simple.

1 he / present / sales report / last Friday .

He presented the sales report last Friday.

2 we / not discuss / prices / yesterday .

_____

3 she / phone Gavin / last week ?

_____

4 they / email you / yesterday ?

_____

5 I / phone Alan / last Monday .

_____

6 she / talk to Sally / yesterday .

_____

5 Match the pairs to make sentences. Write a–j in the boxes.

1 [d] Last year

2 [ ] We travelled by ferry from

3 [ ] We travelled around by

4 [ ] We stayed

5 [ ] Our accommodation

6 [ ] We went sightseeing

7 [ ] Every afternoon we

8 [ ] The nightlife was

9 [ ] There were lots of good

a was near the beach.

b discos and restaurants.

c every morning.

d we went to Spain on holiday.

e relaxed by the pool.

f at a small hotel.

g car.

h very good.

i Plymouth to Santander.

6 Write the past simple form of the verbs.

1 We ___flew___ back last night. *(fly)*

2 I _____ this CD on my holiday. *(buy)*

3 I _____ home last Friday. *(come)*

4 We _____ a ferry to the island. *(take)*

5 We _____ a week in France last year. *(have)*

6 They _____ on May 5th. *(leave)*

7 We _____ at a good restaurant last night. *(eat)*

8 Tom _____ to China last year. *(go)*

9 I _____ a coffee at the airport. *(drink)*

10 The ticket _____ €395. *(cost)*

11 We _____ lots of interesting things. *(see)*

12 We _____ from London to Barcelona. *(drive)*

UNIT 9

1 Match the documents to their definitions.

1 bar chart   a the record of a meeting

2 schedule   b the plan for a meeting

3 agenda   c a circle showing data

4 pie chart   d information in columns

5 minutes   e the timetable for a project

2 Fill in the gaps with the correct object pronouns.

me you him her it us them

1 I don't have the agenda. Could you send ___it___ to me?

2 There's a message for _____ . Can you phone Trevor before 3 pm?

3 Julia wants to see your report. Can you send _____ a copy?

4 I'm sending four attachments. I hope you can open _____ .

5 Mr Johnson phoned. Can you contact _____ today, please?

6 We don't have the new schedule. Can you email it to _____ ?

7 Could you send _____ the minutes for the last meeting? I don't have a copy.

3 Fill in the gaps with the past simple form of the irregular verbs.

1 I ___spoke___ to Roberto yesterday. *(speak)*

2 I _____ John about the meeting. *(tell)*

3 Scott _____ me a copy of the schedule at the last meeting. *(give)*

4 Sarah phoned. She _____ she needs to speak to you. *(say)*

5 I _____ Claire at the conference last week. *(see)*

6 We _____ Sam's presentation was very interesting. *(think)*

7 He _____ my report after the meeting. *(read)*

8 We _____ a planning meeting last Friday *(have)*

9 Tom _____ me an email this morning. *(send)*

10 I _____ a report on the project last month. *(write)*

4 Fill in the gaps in the telephone conversation.

A Could I ¹ ___speak___ to Nathalie, please?

B Who's ² _____ , please?

A ³ _____ 's Jessica Keen.

B Just a ⁴ _____ , please. Would you like to ⁵ _____ ?

A Yes, please.

B Sorry. I'm ⁶ _____ she's not in her office.

A OK, I'll call her ⁷ _____ later.

5 Make offers and decisions using *I'll*.

1 send / you / information .
I'll send you the information.

2 give / Tom / message .

_____

3 phone / you / later .

_____

4 ask / manager / about / order .

_____

5 email / Tina / this morning .

_____

6 call / back / after / meeting .

_____

6 Sense (S) or nonsense (N)? Write S or N in the boxes.

1 Is it warm there? – Yes, it's freezing. ☑ N

2 It's hot and sunny here. ☐

3 It's windy and cloudy in the office this morning. ☐

4 It's freezing this morning. It's minus ten degrees. ☐

5 The weather's miserable here. It's foggy and cold. ☐

6 A What's the weather like there?
B There's a thunderstorm. ☐

7 Circle the correct tense.

1 It _____ every day last month in Moscow.
a is snowing (b) snowed c snows

2 It often _____ in April.
a rains b rained c is raining

3 The sun _____ now.
a shone b shine c is shining

4 We _____ a thunderstorm last night.
a have b had c are having

5 It _____ two days ago.
a is foggy b was foggy

6 It _____ at the moment.
a is windy b was windy

UNIT 10

1 Write the opposites.

small	bad	safe	near	old	cheap
difficult	high				

1 expensive _cheap_

2 low _____

3 large _____

4 dangerous _____

5 easy _____

6 modern _____

7 far _____

8 good _____

2 Make comparisons.

1 planes/trains (+ fast)
Planes are faster than trains.

2 Ferraris/Fords (– economical)
Ferraris are less economical than Fords.

3 driving /flying (+ dangerous)
_____

4 modern jets/older planes (+ safe)
_____

5 Airbus 380/Boeing 747 (+ big)
_____

6 planes/high-speed trains (– reliable)
_____

3 Make superlatives.

1 flying / safe way to travel .
Flying is the safest way to travel.

2 a high-speed train / convenient way to travel .
_____

3 what / good way / get to the airport ?
_____

4 which / expensive airline ?
_____

5 a low-cost airline / cheap option .
_____

4 Fill in the gaps.

sure	right	agree	think	true	prefer

1 A A ticket on the Eurostar costs 200 euros.
B Yes, you're _right_ .

2 A I think trains are the most convenient way to travel.
B Oh, I _____ to drive.

3 A Flying is the best option.
B Yes I _____ .

4 I _____ driving is the most dangerous way to get from A to B.

5 A There are no high-speed trains in England.
B Oh, I'm not so _____ . What about the Intercity?

6 A On short journeys the TGV is faster than flying.
B Yes, that's _____ .

5 Fill in the gaps in the conversation at check-in.

gate   aisle   luggage   briefcase
boarding   delayed   hand   time
passport   card   suitcase

Stewardess	Hello, can I see your ticket and your ¹ *passport* , please?
Passenger	Yes, here's my ticket and I have an identity ² _____ Is that OK?
Stewardess	That's fine, no problem. Would you like an ³ _____ or a window seat?
Passenger	A window seat, please. Is the flight on ⁴ _____ ?
Stewardess	Sorry, no. I'm afraid it's ⁵ _____ about 40 minutes. Do you have any ⁶ _____ to check in?
Passenger	Only one ⁷ _____ .
Stewardess	And do you have any ⁸ _____ luggage?
Passenger	Only my ⁹ _____ .
Stewardess	Yes, that's fine. OK, here's your ¹⁰ _____ pass.
Passenger	Thank you.
Stewardess	Boarding starts in 30 minutes. ¹¹ _____ 42 B.
Passenger	OK, thank you.
Stewardess	You're welcome.

6 Fill in the gaps with *some, any* or *no*.

1 I have _some_ identification – here's my passport.
2 I'm sorry there aren't _____ aisle seats left.
3 I have _____ hand luggage – a briefcase.
4 No, I have _____ luggage.
5 There aren't _____ shops after the security check.
6 There are _____ shops and a café over there.
7 I'm sorry, I have _____ other identification with me.
8 Yes, there's _____ information about flights on the screen over there.

UNIT 11

1 Put the words in order. Make sentences.

1 agenda / shall / the / this / we / afternoon / discuss ?
   Shall we discuss the agenda this afternoon?
2 him / I / the / an / email / send / shall / about / price / new / list ?
   _____
3 meeting / shall / where / have / we / the?
   _____
4 again / let's / on / Friday / afternoon / talk .
   _____
5 shall / when / visit / the / we / factory ?
   _____
6 go / by / to / train / the / let's / conference .
   _____

2 Fill in the gaps.

first   after   urgent   next   finally   then

'¹ _First_ let's have a coffee and ² _____ that we can discuss work. Let's talk about the new office plan, that's the most ³ _____ job, and ⁴ _____ we can discuss the new office furniture. The ⁵ _____ thing to do is to look at suppliers and prices for the furniture. ⁶ _____ , we need to arrange a meeting with the suppliers we choose.'

3 Make sentences with *going to*.

1 where / they / meet ?
   Where are they going to meet?
2 what / she / present / at the conference ?
   _____
3 he / fly / to Moscow / on Friday .
   _____
4 we / have dinner / at the hotel .
   _____
5 you / work / late / tonight ?
   _____
6 I / not book / the tickets / on the Internet .
   _____

4 Fill in the missing letters to complete the sentences.

1 What are your p _l_ _a_ _n_ _s_ for next week?
2 What's your main a _ _ ?
3 Our o _ _i_ _ _ _ _ _ is to make the website easier to use.
4 Our t _ _ _ _ t date is the end of the year.
5 Our g _ _ _ is to finish the project in two months.

5 Make sentences with the correct form of *have got*.

1 Do you have the bill?
 Have you got the bill?
2 We have a reservation for two nights.
 _____
3 Mr Soga doesn't have a minibar in his room.
 _____
4 They don't have their keys.
 _____
5 The receptionist has a message for you.
 _____
6 I don't have your extension number.
 _____

6 Fill in the gaps.

> signature double room extras bill
> wake service check up in minibar

1 Two people need a _double_ room at a hotel.
2 When you arrive at a hotel you _____ _____ .
3 You write your _____ on a cheque.
4 The hotel gives you a _____ when you leave.
5 If you want a meal in your room, phone _____ _____ .
6 You ask for a _____-_____ call, if you need to get up early.
7 Phone calls aren't included in the price of a hotel room. They are _____ .
8 There's a _____ in your room, if you want a drink.

1 Fill in the gaps so that the second sentence in each pair has a similar meaning to the first.

> loss quarter increased profit improved
> costs

1 We earned a lot of money.
 We made a big _profit_ .
2 Here are figures for the last three months.
 Here are figures for the last _____ .
3 We spent less money.
 We cut _____ .
4 Sales grew by 10%.
 Sales _____ by 10%.
5 We lost money last year.
 We made a _____ last year.
6 Our business got better.
 Our business _____ .

2 Change the sentences. Use adverbs.

1 The train is slow.
 The train is travelling _slowly_ .
2 It was a quick meeting.
 The meeting went _____ .
3 We had a good holiday.
 Our holiday went _____ .
4 It's hard work.
 We're working _____ .
5 It was a bad project.
 The project went _____ .
6 She's a fast worker.
 She works _____ .

3 Match the pairs of sentences with similar meanings. Write a–e in the boxes.

1 [c] A lot of companies sell the same products as us.
2 [ ] Lots of people want to buy this.
3 [ ] You can buy this product a bit cheaper.
4 [ ] We have a large stock of products.
5 [ ] We provide the same service as them.

a You can get a small discount.
b We have lots of goods in our warehouse.
c We have lots of competitors.
d We compete with them.
e There's a big demand for it.

4 Make questions with *much* or *many*.

1 how / products / are on sale ?
   How many products are on sale?

2 are / stores / making a profit ?
   _____

3 how / profit / did you make ?
   _____

4 was there / demand / for snacks and drinks ?
   _____

5 how / discount / did you get ?
   _____

6 are / suppliers / selling this product ?
   _____

5 Fill in the gaps.

| pin changing off credit receipt |
| sale size on |

1 They're having a __*sale*__ . Everything is half price.

2 They're half price. There's 50% _____ .

3 The _____ room's just over there.

4 It's too small. Do you have it in a bigger _____ ?

5 A Can I pay by _____ card, please?
   B Yes, of course. Can you put in your _____ number, please?

6 A Is it the right size?
   B I don't know. I'll try it _____ .

7 I'll put your _____ in the bag.

6 Fill in the gaps with *this, that, these* or *those*.

1 Can I try on __*those*__ shoes over there?

2 How much is _____ T-shirt in the shop window?

3 A Do you like _____ shirt?
   B Yes, it looks great on you?!

4 Mmm! _____ sandwiches are delicious!

5 Excuse me. Are _____ jeans over there in the sale?

6 A I've got _____ little present for you. Here you are. Happy birthday!
   B Oh, thanks!

Grammar reference

1 BE: PRESENT SIMPLE

- The verb *be* is irregular.

Positive

long form	short form
I am	I'm
you are	you're
he is	he's
she is	she's
it is	it's
we are	we're
they are	they're

Negatives

long form	short form
I am not	I'm not
you are not	you aren't / you're not
he is not	he isn't / he's not
she is not	she isn't / she's not
it is not	it isn't / it's not
we are not	we aren't / we're not
they are not	they aren't / they're not

Questions	Short answers	
	positive	*negative*
Am I ... ?	Yes, I am.	No, I'm not. (one form)
Are you ... ?	Yes, you are.	No, you aren't / you're not.
Is he ... ?	Yes, he is.	No, he isn't / he's not.
Is she ... ?	Yes, she is.	No, she isn't / she's not.
Is it ... ?	Yes, it is.	No, it isn't / its not.
Are we ... ?	Yes, we are.	No, we aren't / we're not.
Are they ... ?	Yes, they are.	No, they aren't / they're not.

- We use the short form in conversations. *Be* has two negative short forms. They are both common.

2 SUBJECT PRONOUNS

Singular
I/you/he/she *(to talk about people)*
it *(to talk about things and animals)*
Plural
we/you *(to talk about people)*
they *(to talk about people, animals and things)*

- We use pronouns to replace nouns.
  John *is in the office.* › **He** *is in the office.*
  Sally and I *are in London.* › **We** *are in London.*
  Dan and Fergal *are at the sales conference.* › **They** *are at the sales conference.*

- The pronoun *I* always has a capital letter.
  *Tom and **I** are from Boston.*

- *You* is singular and plural.
  *Joe, are **you** from New York?*
  *Ann and Nick, are **you** from New York?*

3 DEFINITE ARTICLE: THE

- There is only one gender for nouns in English, so there is only one definite article: *the.*
  *He is in **the** London office.*
  *St. Petersburg is in **the** north of Russia.*

- We use *the* with singular and plural nouns.
  *Where's **the** office?*
  *Where are **the** offices?*

- We use *the* when we are talking about a particular thing.
  *Close **the** door.*

4 INDEFINITE ARTICLES: A/AN

- There are two indefinite articles: *a* and *an.* We use *a* or *an* with a singular noun.

- We use *a* before consonants:
  ***a** coffee,* ***a** company,* ***a** tea*

- We use *an* before the vowel sounds:
  ***an** apple juice,* ***an** iced tea,* ***an** email,* ***an** office,* ***an** umbrella*

- Some words begin with *u*, but it is not a vowel sound: *a university*.
  H is a consonant, but some words begin with a silent *h*:
  a hotel (consonant)
  an hour (silent *h*)

5 POSSESSIVE ADJECTIVES

- Use these adjectives to talk about possessions.

Singular
my/your/his/her/its
Plural
our/your/their

- The form is the same before a singular or plural noun.
  *What's **his** mobile number?*
  *Where are **his** tickets?*

- We use *his/her* for people. We use *its* for things and animals.
  *Marie is the marketing manager. This is **her** email address.*
  *FJK is a big company. **Its** head office is in Edinburgh.*

6 POSSESSIVE 'S AND OF

- Use the possessive 's with people's names.
  *What's Sally**'s** phone number?*
  (NOT *What's ~~the phone number of Sally?~~*)

- Use the possessive *of* when you talk about places.
  *What's the phone number **of** the factory?*
  (NOT *What's ~~the factory's phone number?~~*)

7 PLURALS

- We use a plural noun to talk about two (or more) persons or things.
  *Two hotdog**s**, please.*
  *The fax**es** are on your desk.*
  *ZY have offic**es** in five countr**ies**.*

- Nouns ending in *-ch*, *-sh*, *-x* or *-s*
  *sandwi**ch** > sandwich**es***
  *fa**x** > fax**es***
  *address > address**es***

- Nouns ending in consonant + *-y*
  *countr**y** > countr**ies***
  *compan**y** > compan**ies***

- There are some irregular plurals (*man > men, woman > women, child > children*).

- When there are two words, only the second word ends in *-s* in the plural.
  *phone number > phone number**s*** (NOT ~~phones numbers~~)

8 QUESTION WORDS

- We use these question words to ask about:

places:	*Where ...?*
things:	*What ...?*
time:	*When ...? / What time ...?*
people:	*Who ...?*
method/way:	*How ...?*
price:	*How much ...?*
number:	*How many ...?*
reason:	*Why ...?*

Where *are you from? – Dijon.*
What's *the address? – It's 52, King Street.*
When's / What time's *the flight to Beijing? – At seven fifteen.*
Who's *the Training Manager? – Matthew Crawford.*
How *do you spell your name? – C-H-R-I-S-S-Y.*
How much *is a coffee? – Two euros.*
How many *people work in your office? – Nine or ten.*
Why *isn't Jenny here? – She's at the Milan office this week.*

(*What's = What is, When's = When is, What time's = What time is, Who's = Who is*)
(See also questions with *much/many*, Grammar reference 34.)

9 PRESENT SIMPLE

- We use the present simple to talk about routines, regular activities and things that are generally true.
  *Helen **works** in Manchester.*
  *I **go** to work by train.*

Positive	
I/you/we/they	work
he/she/it	works
Negative	
I/you/we/they **don't**	work
he/she/it **doesn't**	work

Questions	Short answers
Do I/you/we/they work?	Yes, I/you/we/they **do**. No, I/you/we/they **don't**.
Does he/she/it work?	Yes, he/she/it **does**. No, he/she/it **doesn't**.
(don't = do not, doesn't = does not)	

- For most regular verbs, add an -s to the infinitive to make the third person singular.

  Add -es to *do*, *go*, and verbs ending in *-ch*, *-sh*, *-s* or *-x*.

  For verbs ending in consonant + *-y*, change *-y* to *-ies*.

Infinitive	he/she/it
live	liv**es**
go	go**es**
do	do**es**
watch	watch**es**
fax	fax**es**
supply	suppl**ies**
study	stud**ies**

- For company names we can use the third person singular or the third person plural.

  *Metalin **sell/sells** products all over the world.*

- We use *do* to make questions in the present simple, but *do* is also an ordinary verb.

  *What do you **do**? – I'm an accountant.*

  *She **does** judo at an evening class.*

- Normally we use the short forms (negative) in conversation.

  *He **doesn't** work in an office.*

10 THERE IS/ARE

- We use *there is/are* to say if something exists or how many exist.

- *there's / there is* + singular noun

  ***There's** a car park at the factory. (there's = there is)*

  ***Is there** a cafeteria? – No, **there isn't**.*

- *there are* + plural noun

  ***There are** five computers in the office.*

  ***Are there** power sockets in the room? – No, **there aren't**.*

- The past simple of *there is/are* is *there was/were*.

11 IMPERATIVE

- We use the imperative to give directions, orders and instructions.

- For the positive it is the same as the infinitive. The negative form is: *Don't* + infinitive.

  ***Go** to the end of the corridor. **Turn** left/right.*

  ***Don't use** that computer – it isn't working.*

- In English people mainly use the imperative for directions. It can be very impolite in other situations. For example, it is much more polite to say *'Could I have a coffee, please?'* than *'Give me a coffee, please'*.

12 ADJECTIVES

- Adjectives go before the noun they describe (or after the verb *be*).

  *It's a **new** computer.*

  *This computer is **new**.*

- Adjectives have only one form for singular and plural.

  *It's a **big** house with a **small** garden.*

  *They are **big** houses with **small** gardens.*

- We use *quite* and *very* before an adjective to describe something in more detail.

His office is	very big.
	quite big.
	not very big.
	quite small.
	very small.

- We can also use *really* and *fairly* in this way.

  *This meeting is **really** important. (= very)*

  *It's **fairly** expensive. (= quite)*

13 PREPOSITIONS

Location:

- Use *in* and *near* for location of a town/city.

  *Madrid is **in** Spain, **in** the centre.*

  *Canton is **near** Hong Kong.*

Time:

- Use *the ... of* with dates:

  ***the** tenth **of** June*

- Use *on* for a specific day or date:

  ***on** Saturday / New Year's Day / 15th March*

- Use *in* for a period of time:
  in June / the first quarter / 2006

- Use *at* with clock times and parts of weeks or months:
  at ten o'clock / the end of June / the weekend
  BUT: *in the middle of April*

- For parts of the day we say:
  in the morning/afternoon/evening
  BUT: *at night*

14 CAN

- We use *can* to ask permission and make requests.

  Permission:
  Can I use your phone?

  Requests:
  Can you photocopy this, please?

  (See also *could* for permission and requests, Grammar reference 15.)

- We also use *can* to talk about possibility and ability.

  Possibility:
  You **can't** buy it in the shops, but you **can** order it on the Internet.

  Ability:
  He **can** speak Chinese, but he **can't** write it.

- There is only one form of this verb for all persons.

  Positive: subject + *can* + infinitive
  I **can** open this file.

  Negative: subject + *can't* + infinitive
  She **can't** use a computer.

  Questions: *Can* + subject + infinitive
  Can we pay by credit card?

  Short answers: *Yes/No* + subject + *can/can't*
  Yes, you **can.**/No, you **can't.**

- In the negative there is also long form *(cannot)*. Normally, we use the short form *(can't)*. The long form is very formal.

- We use *You can ...* to mean 'people in general'.
  You **can** book your ticket online.

15 COULD

- We use *could* to ask permission and make polite requests. It is more polite than *can*.

  Permission:
  Could I use your phone?

  Requests:
  Could you photocopy this, please?

- There is only one form of this verb for all persons. In questions the form is:

  Could + subject + infinitive
  Could you say that again, please?
  (NOT ~~Could you to say that again, please?~~)

16 NEED (TO)

- We use *need* in two different ways, to talk about things which are necessary.

  need + *to* + infinitive
  I **need to** read the report before the meeting.
  need + noun
  He **needs** 20 copies of the report.

17 ADVERBS OF FREQUENCY

- We use adverbs of frequency (*often*, *sometimes*, *never*, etc.) with verbs to say how often people do things.

- Adverbs of frequency generally go before the main verb, but after the verb *be*.
  I **always go** to the sales conference.
  We **never give** presentations.
  Our profits **are usually** very good.

- We also use *a lot/lots* to mean *often*.
  He travels abroad **a lot**.

18 PRESENT CONTINUOUS (FOR THE PRESENT)

- We use this tense to describe things that are happening now / at the moment.
  Where's Nick? – He**'s having** lunch at the moment.
  They**'re visiting** our new factory this week.
  I**'m working** at home today.

- The form of the present continuous is:
  be + verb + *-ing*.

Positive

I'm	
he's/she's/ it's	going.
you're/we're/ they're	

Negative

I'm not working

he/she/it	isn't / 's not	
you/we/they	aren't / 're not	going.

Questions

Am I	
Is he/she/it	going?
Are you/we/they	

Short answers

positive

Yes, I am.

Yes, he/she it is.

Yes, you/we/they are.

negative

No, I'm not.

No, he/she/it	isn't / 's not.
No, you/we/they	aren't / 're not.

- If the infinitive of the verb ends in *-e*, remove the *-e* before adding *-ing*.

  mak**e** > mak**ing**

  phon**e** > phon**ing**

  hav**e** > hav**ing**

- With some verbs you double the last consonant.

  run > ru**nn**ing

  swim > swi**mm**ing

  travel > trave**ll**ing

19 GERUND

- We use a verb + *-ing* (or an ordinary noun) after verbs of like and dislike (for example, *like/love/hate/prefer/don't mind*)

  I love **swimming**.

  He likes **travelling** but he doesn't like long flights.

20 PRESENT CONTINUOUS: FUTURE ARRANGEMENTS

- We use the present continuous to talk about definite arrangements for the future.

  She**'s presenting** the new product on Friday.

  I**'m going** to Milan next week.

  (See Grammar reference 18, for the form.)

21 *WOULD LIKE TO*

- We use *would like to* to ask polite questions. It is more polite than *want to*. The negative form of *would* is *wouldn't*.

  Would you **like to** reserve a seat? – Yes, **I would**. / No, **I wouldn't**.

- The positive form is *would like to* + infinitive. We normally use the short form of *would* (*'d*) when we speak.

  I**'d like to** travel second class, please. (= I would like to)

22 *BE*: PAST SIMPLE

Positive

I/he/she/it was

you/we/they were

Negative

I/he/she/it wasn't

you/we/they weren't

Questions

Was I/he/she/it ...?

Were you/we/they ...?

Short answers

positive

Yes, I/he/she/it was.

Yes, you/we/they were.

negative

No, I/he/she/it wasn't.

No, you/we/they weren't.

- *Wasn't* and *weren't* are short forms for *was not* and *were not*. We normally use the short forms of the negative in conversation.

- With *be*, no auxiliary verb is needed in the past simple:

  Was he late?

  NOT ~~Did was he late?~~

23 PAST SIMPLE

- The form for the past simple is the same for all persons. Most regular verbs follow the same pattern.

  Positive: subject + infinitive + -ed
  He **talked** to Ben yesterday.

  Negative: subject + didn't + infinitive
  They **didn't discuss** the report.

  Question: Did + subject + infinitive
  Did you **talk** about the trip to China?

  Short answers: Yes/No + subject did/didn't.
  Yes, I **did**. / No, I **didn't**.

- For verbs ending in -e, just add -d, to make the positive form.

  phon**e**
  I phon**ed** him, but he was in a meeting.
  receiv**e**
  We receiv**ed** your order last Monday.

- For verbs ending in consonant + -y, change -y to -ied.
  suppl**y**
  Last year we suppl**ied** all their stores.
  stud**y**
  She stud**ied** German for two years.

24 OBJECT PRONOUNS

- We use object pronouns when we don't want to repeat the names of people or things. Object pronouns go after the main verb or after a preposition.
  I can speak to Ms Jones. I'm seeing **her** today.
  Do you have the agenda? – Yes, I have **it**.
  Jim and Rosa are here. I'm working with **them**.

- In English there is no difference between direct object and indirect object pronouns.
  Peter, could you send **me** the schedule? (indirect object = to me)
  I sent **it** last week. (direct object)
  He needs the file. Can you send it to **him**? (indirect object)
  Can you check the figures and send **them** to Kelly? (direct object)

25 *WILL*: SPONTANEOUS DECISIONS AND OFFERS

- Use *will* when you offer or quickly decide to do something:
  Can I give you the number? – Yes, **I'll** write it down.
  Antonio's having lunch. – OK, **I'll** call back later.
  The photocopier isn't working. – Right, **we'll** send someone to repair it.

- The short form of *will* is *'ll* (*I'll* = *I will*, *you'll* = *you will*, etc.) Always use the short form when you speak, for offers and decisions.

26 COMPARATIVES

- When you compare two things use the comparative form + *than*.
  Modern planes are **bigger than** older ones.
  Business class is **more expensive than** economy class.

- There are two different ways to make the positive comparative form of regular adjectives:
  – adjective + -er
  – more + adjective
  The form you use depends on the number of syllables in the adjective.

- For one-syllable adjectives ending in a consonant, add -er:
  small › small**er**   cheap › cheap**er**
  fast › fast**er**
  (Some short adjectives double the final consonant: big › bi**gg**er)

- If a one-syllable adjective already ends in -e, you just add -r:
  saf**e** › safe**r**   nic**e** › nice**r**   larg**e** › large**r**

- If a two-syllable adjective ends in -y, take away the -y and add -ier:
  bus**y** › bus**ier**   eas**y** › eas**ier**

- If a two-syllable adjective ends in a consonant, use *more* + adjective:
  modern › **more** modern
  formal › **more** formal

- With long adjectives of three or more syllables, use *more* + adjective:
  expensive › **more** expensive
  economical › **more** economical

- There is only one negative comparative form: *less* + adjective:

  less *cheap*   **less** *busy*   **less** *modern*
  less *expensive*

- There is no pattern to irregular adjectives. You have to learn the different forms of the comparative. (See Unit 10.1.)

27 SUPERLATIVES

- There are two different ways to make the superlative form of regular adjectives:

  – *the* + adjective + *-est*

  – *the* + *more/less* + adjective

  As for the comparative, the form you use depends on the number of syllables in the adjective.

- For one-syllable adjectives ending in a consonant, add *-est* :

  small > *the small**est**   cheap* > *the cheap**est**
  fast* > *the fast**est***

  (Some short adjectives double the final consonant: *big* > *big**g**est*)

- If a one-syllable adjective already ends in *-e*, you just add *-st*:

  safe > *the saf**est**   nice* > *the nic**est**
  large* > *the larg**est***

- If a two-syllable adjective ends in *-y*, take away the *-y* and add *-iest*:

  busy > *the bus**iest**   easy* > *the eas**iest***

  If a two-syllable adjective ends in a consonant, use *the most* + adjective:

  modern > *the **most** modern*
  formal > *the **most** formal*

- With long adjectives of three or more syllables, use *the most* + adjective:

  expensive > *the **most** expensive*
  economical > *the **most** economical*

- There is only one negative comparative form: *the least* + adjective:

  *the **least** cheap*   *the **least** busy*
  *the **least** modern*   *the **least** expensive*

- There is no pattern to irregular adjectives. You have to learn the different forms of the superlative. (See Unit 10.2.)

28 SOME/ANY/NO

(See countable/uncountable nouns, Grammar reference 33.)

- Use *any* with uncountable or plural nouns in questions.

  *Do you have **any** identification/luggage?*
  *Are there **any** shops / window seats?*

- Use *any* with uncountable or plural nouns in negative sentences.

  *I **don't** have **any** luggage.*
  *I **don't** have **any** bags.*

- Use *some* with uncountable or plural nouns in positive sentences.

  *I have **some** identification/luggage.*
  *There are **some** shops/suitcases there.*

- Use *no* with uncountable or plural nouns to say that you don't have something.

  *I have **no** luggage.*
  *I have **no** bags.*

29 SUGGESTIONS: *SHALL I/WE …?   LET'S … .*

- We use *shall* and *let's* to make suggestions. Their form is:

  Shall + *I/we* + infinitive?

  Let's + infinitive

- Use *Shall I …?* when you offer to do something or suggest doing something.

  Offer:
  ***Shall I** do the photocopies?*
  Suggestion:
  ***Shall I** write the report now?*

- Use *Shall we …?* when you want to suggest doing something with someone else.

  ***Shall we** meet next week?*
  ***Shall we** talk about the design?*

- Use *Let's … .* when you want to suggest doing something with someone else.

  ***Let's** catch the ten o'clock train.*
  ***Let's** go to the Berlin trade fair.*

  Let's is the short form of *Let us*. Always use the short form – the long form is uncommon.

30 FUTURE WITH *GOING TO*

- We use *going to* to talk about plans and intentions.

- The form is: *be* + *going to* + infinitive.

Positive

I'm		
He's/She's/It's	going to	start early.
You're/We're/They're		

Negative

I'm not		
He/She/It isn't	going to	start early.
You/We/They aren't		

Questions

Am I		
Is he/she/it	going to	start early?
Are you/we/they		

Short answers

positive	*negative*
Yes, I am.	No, I'm not.
Yes, he/she/it is.	No, he/she/it isn't.
Yes, you/we/they are.	No, you/we/they aren't.

31 HAVE GOT

- In British English *have got* is a very common variant of the verb *have* (when it refers to possession). It is used very often when people speak. Usually people use the short form – the long form is uncommon.

  She**'s got** a new job.

  We **haven't got** time to discuss it now.

  Have you **got** Caroline's email address?

Positive

I've/You've/We've/They've got a new address.

He's/She's/It's got a new address.

Negative

I/You/We/They haven't got a new address.

He/She/It hasn't got a new address.

Questions

Have I/you/we/they got a new address?

Has he/she/it got a new address?

Short answers

positive

Yes, I/you/we/they have.

Yes, he/she/it has.

negative

No, I/you/we/they haven't.

No, he/she/it hasn't.

- We don't use *have got* with meals/drinks/snacks or shower/bath.

  I usually have breakfast at seven o'clock.

  (NOT ~~I've usually got breakfast at eleven o'clock.~~)

32 ADVERBS OF MANNER

- We use adverbs of manner to describe actions (how people do things).

  *She talks very **quickly**.*

  *He works **hard**.*

  (See Unit 12.1 for the form of regular and irregular adverbs.)

- Adverbs of manner usually come after the verb.

  *It's falling **quickly**.*

  *It increased **slowly**.*

33 COUNTABLE AND UNCOUNTABLE NOUNS

- Most nouns are countable (they have a plural form and you can count them).

  a computer > two computers

  an email > some emails

- Some nouns are uncountable (they do not have a plural form).

  (some) information/luggage/news/competition

  (NOT ~~an information~~)

- Use a singular verb with uncountable nouns.

  *There's some **information** about flights on the screen.*

  (See also some/any/no, and questions with much/many, Grammar reference 28 and 34.)

34 QUESTIONS WITH MUCH/MANY

- We use *how much* and *how many* in questions about quantity and number.

- We use *much* with uncountable nouns to ask about quantity.

  *Is there **much** demand for this product?*

- We also use *how much* to ask about price.

  ***How much** is a hamburger? – Two pounds fifty.*

- We use *many* with countable nouns to talk about number.

  ***How many** competitors do you have? – About five or six for this market.*

  (See also countable and uncountable nouns, Grammar reference 33.)

35 *THIS/THESE, THAT/THOSE*

- We use *this/these* to talk about things which are very near or in our hands.

  *Is **this** your pen?*

- We use *that/those* to talk about things which are not near or which we point at.

  ***That's** my car, over there.*

  *I like **those** bracelets in the shop window.*

- *This/that* refer to singular nouns. *These/Those* refer to plural nouns.

- We sometimes use *this/that* to talk about people.

  *Who's **that**?*

  *Martin, **this** is my colleague, Jenny.*

IRREGULAR VERBS

Infinitive	Past simple		Infinitive	Past simple
be	was/were		learn	learned/learnt
become	became		leave	left
begin	began		lose	lost
break	broke		make	made
bring	brought		meet	met
build	built		pay	paid
buy	bought		put	put
catch	caught		read	read /red/
choose	chose		ring	rang
come	came		run	ran
cost	cost		say	said
cut	cut		see	saw
do	did		sell	sold
draw	drew		send	sent
drink	drank		sing	sang
drive	drove		sleep	slept
eat	ate		speak	spoke
fall	fell		spend	spent
feel	felt		stand	stood
find	found		swim	swam
fly	flew		take	took
forget	forgot		teach	taught
get	got		tell	told
give	gave		think	thought
go	went		throw	threw
have	had		understand	understood
hear	heard /hɜːd/		wake	woke
keep	kept		wear	wore
know	knew		win	won
			write	wrote

Transcripts

▶▶ 4

1 UPS 2 IBM 3 AOL 4 RNX Auto 5 TDK 6 ZY Systems 7 VW 8 GEC 9 JFK Cargo 10 Snack HQ

▶▶ 7

1 I'm Brad Carrington. I'm from the USA.
2 Hello. I'm Hans Schwartz. I'm from Germany.
3 Hi. Jan Grabowski, from Poland.
4 I'm Maria Gonzales and I'm from Spain.
5 I'm Shen Lin, from China. Nice to meet you.
6 I'm Nathalie Lemaire. I'm from France.
7 Hi. I'm Pedro da Silva. I'm from Brazil.
8 Hello. I'm Alison Smith, from the UK.

▶▶ 10

1 A coffee, please.
2 An orange juice, please.
3 Could I have an iced tea, please?
4 An apple juice, please.
5 Um … a tea, please.
6 Could I have a mineral water, please?

▶▶ 11

Joe   Would you like a drink, Claire?
Claire Yes, please. Could I have a tea?
Joe   Yes. Milk? Sugar?
Claire With milk, please. No sugar.
Joe   OK. And Anne?
Anne   Could I have an orange juice, please?
Joe   Sure.

▶▶ 13

zero, one, two, three, four, five, six, seven, eight, nine, ten

▶▶ 14

1 A What's your telephone number?
  B Zero two eight six, one zero four, four nine three.
  A Zero two eight six, one zero four, four nine three?
  B That's right.

2 A My phone number's two one two …
  B Sorry?
  A Two one two.
  B Right.
  A Six three seven, four eight five nine.
  B So, two one two, six three seven, four eight five nine.
  A That's right.

3 A So, your phone number is oh one six three two, seven five four, nine double six.
  B Yes.
  A OK.

4 A What's your number?
  B My phone number?
  A Yes.
  B Oh seven nine eight …
  A Five eight?
  B No, *nine* eight.
  A Right.
  B Two five one …
  A Sorry?
  B Two five one.
  A Right.
  B Three seven four six.
  A OK. So, oh seven nine eight, two five one, three seven, four six.
  A That's right.

▶▶ 16

A My phone number's oh one six one, nine three eight, four five two seven.
B Zero one six one, nine three eight, four five two seven.
A That's right. And my mobile number is oh double seven, nine one, double oh, three four six.
B Zero seven seven, nine one zero zero, three four six. … And your fax number?
A Um … It's oh one six one, nine three nine, eight double two, three.
B Zero one, six one, nine three nine, eight, two two three.
A That's right.
B OK. Thanks, Richard.
A No problem.

▶▶ 17

1 r dot cane at orange dash design dot com
2 service at c c s dot f r
3 k dash suzuki at east dot j p
4 f underscore carlton at netgate dot co dot u k
5 prince underscore one at c n v dot d e
6 smirnov at u dash mail dot r u

▶▶ 18

eleven, twelve, thirteen, fourteen, fifteen, sixteen, seventeen, eighteen, nineteen, twenty, thirty, forty, fifty, fifty-one

▶▶ 19

thirteen, thirty
fourteen, forty
fifteen, fifty

▶▶ 20

1 The fourteen thirteen flight to Frankfurt Main is now ready for boarding …
2 The fourteen twenty departure, flight AA one one one to Rome is …
3 British Airways, flight zero zero nine seven, departing at fourteen thirty-five to London Heathrow is …
4 … flight to Mexico City, due to depart at fourteen forty-eight, will now depart at 15.30 …

5 The fifteen twelve departure to Madrid, flight number IB seven six one three is now ready ...

6 The fifteen eighteen departure to Toronto Pearson, flight number AA ...

▶▶ 21

1 nine am / nine o'clock in the morning
2 midday/noon
3 three pm / three o'clock in the afternoon
4 seven pm / seven o'clock in the evening
5 eleven pm / eleven o'clock at night
6 midnight
7 one pm / one o'clock in the afternoon
8 five am / five o'clock in the morning

▶▶ 22

1 A What's the time?
  B It's quarter past eleven.

2 A What time is it?
  B It's ten past twelve.

3 A What's the time?
  B It's five to eight.

4 A What time is it?
  B It's quarter to five.

5 A Excuse me. What's the time?
  B It's half past nine.

▶▶ 24

sixty   seventy   eighty   ninety   a hundred

▶▶ 25

1 In Brazil, a Big Mac is one dollar sixty-five.
2 A How much is a Big Mac in France?
  B Two euros eighty-two.
3 A Big Mac is two dollars seventy-eight in Japan.
4 In Switzerland, a Big Mac is three dollars forty-eight.
5 A How much is a Big Mac in the UK?
  B In pounds?
  A Yeah.
  B One pound ninety.

▶▶ 26

tomato, salad, chips, beef, chicken, hotdog, burger, tuna, egg, cheese

▶▶ 27

1 A Could I have a burger, please?
  B Anything else?
  A Um ... yes, and a tea, please.
  B That's four euros sixty-five, please.
  A Four ... sixty-five.
  B Thanks.

2 A Two hotdogs, please.
  B Two?
  A Yes, please. And two coffees. How much is that?
  B Um ... eight seventy.
  A OK, eight dollars seventy.

3 A Two tuna sandwiches, please. And a cheese sandwich.
  B Anything else?
  A No, thanks.
  B OK. That's seven pounds eighty.

▶▶ 31

1 A So, you're here on business?
  B Yeah. I work for a consulting company. Santia Partners.
  A And what do you do?
  B I'm an accountant.
  A Right.
  B I work at the office in Mexico City.
  A OK. So is it an international company, Santia?

2 B So, what company do you work for?
  A Irex Chemicals. I'm an engineer.
  B OK. And where do you work?
  A In a factory in Boston.
  B Right. And do you live in Boston?
  A Yes. I live near the coast, not far from ...

▶▶ 34

four hundred, eight hundred and fifty, sixty-five thousand, two hundred and seventy thousand, three point two million, six point eight billion

▶▶ 37

Frank At this factory, we make steel products. And at the other factory in Munich, they make products from aluminium.
Jane Right. Where does your steel come from?
Frank Where do we buy it?
Jane Yeah.
Frank From a supplier here, in Hamburg.
Jane Right. And does it come from Germany?
Frank No. It comes from China. Our supplier is an importer.
Jane OK.
Frank We buy about two hundred and fifty tonnes a year. So we're only a small buyer. But ... with two hundred and fifty tonnes of steel, we make twelve thousand products.
Jane Right. So you make twelve thousand products a year at this factory. Where do you sell your products?
Frank We sell fifteen percent of them in Germany, and ... the other eighty-five percent ... all over the world. We have customers in ... twenty-two countries.
Jane Huh, OK.
Frank In the UK, we sell a lot of equipment to a company in ...

▶▶ 38

1 Where does your steel come from?
2 Where do we buy it?
3 Does it come from Germany?
4 Where do you sell your products?

▶▶ 39

1 A What time do you get up in the morning?
  B Quarter past six.
2 I have breakfast at half past seven.
3 A What time do you start work?
  B At nine o'clock.
4 I have lunch at twelve thirty.
5 A Do you have a break in the afternoon?
  B Yes, we have a break at three o'clock.
6 A What time do you finish work?
  B I finish at five thirty.
7 A When do you have dinner?
  B At about half past seven.

▶▶ 40

A Good morning.
B Morning. Sorry I'm late.
A Oh, you're not late. It's only five past eight.
B Five minutes late.
A No problem. Would you like a coffee?
B Oh, yes please. Five past eight. It isn't late for me, it's early!
A What time do you start work then?
B Nine o'clock. I'm not a morning person!
A We start at seven thirty.
B Seven thirty!
A But we don't work late … . We aren't evening people!
B My boss isn't a morning person or an evening person! He starts at nine and finishes at four … . But he doesn't have lunch.
A Right. He doesn't have time!
B No!

▶▶ 43

1 In Spain, we have dinner at nine or ten o'clock in the evening. When my colleagues come here from other countries, they say we eat late. They're quite surprised.
2 In hotels in the UK, they serve bacon and eggs for breakfast, so a lot of people from other countries think that's the normal English breakfast. But, in fact, at home, most British people don't have bacon and eggs in the morning. They just have cereal or toast … just a light breakfast. And then they have lunch at twelve or twelve thirty.
3 In France, we have an hour, an hour and a half, two hours for lunch. It depends on the company you work for. But people like to have a … a good break at lunchtime. Lunch is an important meal in France.
4 In the United States, we don't have long lunch breaks. A lot of people just stop work for half an hour and have a sandwich in the office. People prefer to have a short break at lunchtime, and finish work early.

5 Here in Switzerland, people start work at … half past seven, eight o'clock. And we like to have a good breakfast before we go to work, so we get up, um … quite early.
6 In Japan, a lot of managers have dinner in the evening, then they go back to the office and work until nine or … or ten o'clock. Or later, sometimes.

▶▶ 44

Neil Hello Tina, it's Neil.
Tina Hi, Neil.
Neil Tina, I have a question.
Tina Mmm.
Neil It's about the sales report. I don't understand an abbreviation on page six. It says 'We need to invest in the B2B market'.
Tina B2B?
Neil Yeah – letter B, number two, letter B. It's sales jargon. What does it mean?
Tina B2B … Good question. I don't know. Er … Is it, um … Does B stand for 'business'? Does it mean 'business-to-business'?
Neil Oh, so the 'two' means 'to'. Yeah … maybe …
Tina Do you know, um … NetLingo? The website?
Neil No.
Tina It has a dictionary of … Internet business jargon, …
Neil Oh, right. What's the address?
Tina I'm not sure, but I think it's netlingo dot com.
Neil How do you spell 'netlingo'?
Tina N-E-T-L-I-N-G-O.
Neil Netlingo dot com. OK, thanks very much Tina.
Tina No problem.

▶▶ 45

Customer My name's Linda Sammerson. And I'm from Hughes Insurance.
Neil Sorry? Could you say that again?
Customer Linda Sammerson. S-A double M-E-R-S-O-N.
Neil Could you speak more slowly, please?
Customer Sorry. S-A double M-E-R-S-O-N.
Neil S-A-double M-E-R-S-O-N.
Customer That's right. And I'm from Hughes Insurance.
Neil Hughes? Could you spell that, please?
Customer H-U-G-H-E-S.
Neil H-U-G-H-E-S.
Customer That's right.
Neil OK. Well, thanks very much for your call. I'll check …

▶▶ 50

Sue Stephan?
Stephan Yeah?
Sue Can I buy train tickets for France here in the UK?
Stephan Yeah. You can book on the Internet.
Sue Right.
Stephan At SNCF dot com.

Sue	SNCF – that's the French train company?
Stephan	Yeah. Do you need to book a ticket?
Sue	I'm not sure. Possibly. So is this website just in French, or is it …?
Stephan	No, you can choose English.
Sue	And can you pay by credit card?
Stephan	Yeah, and they send the tickets by mail.
Sue	To your home address?
Stephan	Yeah.
Sue	You can't receive tickets if you live in the UK, though …
Stephan	Yes, you can. They send tickets to different countries.
Sue	Oh, right. So SNCF dot com, then.
Stephan	That's right.
Sue	OK, thanks.
Stephan	No problem.

▶▶ 53

(Rec = Receptionist)

Customer	So, there are meeting rooms at the hotel.
Rec	Yes, we have a business centre with four rooms.
Customer	Right. So for a meeting with three people, um …
Rec	Oh yes, that's no problem. There are six chairs in each room, so …
Customer	OK. That's fine, then.
Rec	Then in reception there's a photocopier, if you need to make copies.
Customer	Right.
Rec	There's a fax machine, um … a drinks machine … Do you need a telephone?
Customer	Er, no.
Rec	OK. It's just we don't have phones in the rooms. Most people have mobiles, so …
Customer	Of course, yeah. No, that's no problem. Er … Just a question about computers. Um …
Rec	We don't have computers, I'm afraid.
Customer	No, no, that's OK. It's just I have a laptop. Um …
Rec	Oh, I see.
Customer	Are there power sockets?
Rec	Yes.
Customer	Great. And is there a phone socket, for an Internet connection? So I can send emails.
Rec	Um … We don't have phone sockets in the meeting rooms, so … no. Um …
Customer	Well, no. It's not a problem. I can connect to the phone socket in the bedroom.
Rec	Oh, yes. The bedrooms all have phones, so …
Customer	OK. That's fine then. Um … OK, so can I book …

▶▶ 55

1 A I need to photocopy this. Could I use the photocopier?
  B Yes, sure.
2 A I need to phone my assistant. Can I make a phone call from here?
  B Yes, go ahead.
3 A I need to fax this to my office. Could I use the fax machine?
  B Yes, of course.
4 A I need to email this file. Can I send emails from this computer?
  B Yes, no problem.
5 A I need to print a copy of this file. Is there a printer I can use?
  B Yes, sure.

▶▶ 58

1 Where's the lift, please?
2 Where are the stairs, please?
3 Excuse me. Where's the exit?
4 Excuse me. Where are the toilets?

▶▶ 59

1 A Excuse me, where's the exit?
  B The exit?
  A Yeah.
  B It's just over there. Go to the end of the corridor, then turn left …
2 A Are there toilets on this floor?
  B Yes. They're in the corridor. If you go out of the office, through …
3 A Is there a lift?
  B Sorry?
  A Is there a lift?
  B Yes, there is. It's just past the stairs …
4 A Are you lost?
  B Um … yes. Where are the stairs?
  A They're just through the doors. If you go through those …

▶▶ 60

1 A Excuse me. Where's the lift?
  B It's over there. The first door on the right.
2 A Excuse me. Where are the stairs?
  B On the right, just after the lift.
  A OK. Thanks.
3 A Where's the computer room?
  B It's just past the stairs. The third door on the right.
  A Oh right. Thanks.
4 A Where's the drinks machine?
  B Go to the end of the corridor, through the doors, and turn left.
5 A Where are the toilets, please?
  B Go through the doors at the end, and they're on the right.
  A OK.

▶▶ 62

1 house 2 apartment 3 kitchen 4 bedroom
5 living room 6 bathroom 7 garden

▶▶ 63

A So, do you live near the office?
B Yeah. My house is about … six, seven kilometres from here.
A Oh, so you live in a house. Not an apartment.
B Yeah. It's quite small. Just two bedrooms.
A Yeah.
B But, you know, it's near the centre of town, so …
A Yeah, that's good. Does it have a garden?
B Um …
A You're not sure!
B There *is* a garden, but it's, um … *very* small. It's about twenty-five square metres!
A Right.
B There's just a bin!
A OK.
B It's quite an old property, but, um … it's OK, you know. The problem here is property prices are crazy.
A Expensive?
B Oh, yeah. Very. Over the last … four, five years …

▶▶ 64

1 I have a lot of meetings. Um … they're usually here in the office. Not big meetings. There are usually … four, five, six people.
2 I don't often give big presentations, um … to large numbers of people. They're often just to small groups.
3 Our company has a conference every year. Um … so I always go to that. But that's the only conference I go to.
4 I never go to trade fairs in other countries. But I go to two or three in this country.
5 We have a branch in Brussels, so I sometimes go to the office there. Um … that's all, really. I don't go on a lot of business trips.

▶▶ 65

Interviewer So, you're a television producer? Is that right?
Veronica Um … What's my job title? That's a good question!
Interviewer You make TV programmes, basically.
Veronica Yeah, I usually work for television companies in Japan – for Japanese TV channels. And I make programmes about … the UK. About life in the UK.
Interviewer So you live and work here in the UK, and you make all your programmes here.
Veronica That's right.
Interviewer And are the programmes in Japanese?
Veronica Yes. The TV presenters are always from Japan. Um … The programmes are never in English.
Interviewer And the production team? The cameraman and …
Veronica Um … it depends. We sometimes work with a team from Japan, sometimes it's a team from the UK. It depends on the TV channel. But the presenter is always Japanese.
Interviewer And do you often go to Japan, on business?
Veronica Um … sometimes, yeah. For big programmes, before we start production, I go to Tokyo, and … and I have meetings with colleagues … at the TV companies. But I don't go very often. Um … We sometimes talk on the phone, but … but not a lot, really. The problem with phone calls is the time difference. You know, if it's lunchtime in the UK, it's ten o'clock in the evening in Japan. So … we send a lot of emails.
Interviewer And do you travel a lot in the UK?
Veronica Oh, yeah. Yeah. I go all over the country.
Interviewer So what subjects are the programmes about? You say 'life in the UK'.
Veronica Yeah, um … there are lots of subjects. Er … London buses, the Loch Ness Monster, er … music, property, er …

▶▶ 66

Jacky Good meeting, Stuart?
Stuart Yeah, OK. But a bit long. Five hours!
Jacky *Five* hours?
Stuart Yeah. I don't have a lot of meetings, but when I do …
Jacky They're long.
Stuart Yeah.
Jacky Do you have a lot of meetings at head office?
Stuart No, I don't often go to head office, now. I don't travel a lot, really. I never go abroad on business.
Jacky No?
Stuart No. I don't need to. With the new job, it's … it's just phone calls and emails. A lot of phone calls!

▶▶ 70

1 A Hello. Is Steve there, please?
  B No, he's having lunch at the moment.
  A OK, no problem. I can call back later.

2 A Hello.
  B Hello, Olivia. It's Rick.
  A Hi, Rick. Can I phone you later? I'm driving.
  B Yes, OK.

3 A Could I speak to Colin, please?
  B He's having a meeting this morning.
  A Oh, right.

4 A Hi, it's Mitch. Is Nadia there?
  B No, she's not here, Mitch. She's visiting a customer this week in Australia.
  B Australia!
  A Yeah.

5 Hello, this is Paolo Constantine's extension. I'm not in the office at present. I'm working on a project abroad. Please send me an email if you need to contact me urgently. Thank you.

6 A Could I speak to Sylvia Jarvis, please?
   B She isn't in the office today. She's working at home.
   A Oh.
   B She's here on Monday.
   A Right. OK, I can call on Monday, then. Thanks.

▶▶ 72

A There's a nice swimming pool here.
B Here at the hotel?
A Yeah. In the basement. It's quite big.
B Oh. Well I'm not going in it.
A Don't you like swimming?
B I hate swimming!
A Oh, I love swimming. It's good for you, as well.
B Not if you can't swim!
A No, that's true!
B Do you often go?
A Swimming?
B Yeah.
A Quite often, yeah. I go running quite a lot as well.
   I don't like it, though!
B No, I don't like running.
A Do you go?
B No. No, I don't like sports. I go walking, sometimes.
   Oh, and I like skiing.
A Yeah?
B Yeah. I don't go very often. Just ..., you know, on
   holiday.
A So, are you good?
B Yeah, I'm quite good.
A I'm ... not very good at skiing ...

▶▶ 73

1 A So, what do you do when you're not at work?
   B Um ... I play basketball.
   A Basketball?
   B Yeah, I'm in a local team.
   A Right.
   B I do aerobics, as well. Um ... What about you?
   A I go cycling sometimes.
   B Oh, I go cycling as well.
   A Right.
   B Yeah. Where do you go?
   A Er ...

2 A So, you play football?
   B I play football, I do weight training two or three
      times a week, I go fishing ...
   A What sort of fish do you catch?
   B Big ones! I have some photos I can show you ...

3 A So, what do you do in your spare time?
   B Um ... I play chess, um ... I play the guitar.
   A Oh. Are you good?
   B At chess or the guitar? Well, actually I'm not very
      good at either, so ...
   A Right!

B I go running.
A Yeah.
B What about you?
A Um ..., well ...

▶▶ 74

1 A So, we need to have a meeting about this new
      project.
   B Yeah.
   A When can we meet? I'm free at the end of January.
   B The *end* of January? Um ... yeah.
   A What about the twenty-eighth?
   B Um ... Yes, I can make it on the twenty-eighth.
   A OK. The twenty-eighth of January, then.

2 A I'm free in February. Can we visit the factory then?
   B I'm busy at the beginning of February. What about
      the last week in February?
   A Yeah.
   B Monday the twenty-second?
   A Yes, that's fine.

3 A So, for our next meeting, um ... are you free in
      the middle of March?
   B What date?
   A What about the twelfth?
   B Friday the twelfth?
   A Yes.
   B No, I can't make it on Friday. What about the
      Monday after? Monday the fifteenth?
   A Yes, OK.
   B Right. So, Monday the fifteenth.

4 A We need to arrange a date for the meeting.
   B Yes. Um ...
   A Can you make it on the fifth of April?
   B Yes. I'm free on the fifth. What time?
   A In the morning?
   B Yeah.
   A At nine o'clock?
   B OK. Yes, that's fine.
   A OK. So the fifth of April at nine am.

▶▶ 76

1 I can't make it on Wednesday morning.
2 The meeting's on Monday.
3 Are you free on Tuesday?
4 I'm not here on Friday afternoon.
5 I'm going cycling on Sunday.
6 I'm busy on Thursday.
7 I'm working on Saturday morning.

▶▶ 79

Lilly When are you going to Europe, Gary? Next week?
Gary   Yes. I'm leaving Los Angeles on Monday.
Lilly Where are you going? To the London office?
Gary   Yes.
Lilly Uhuh. Who are you meeting? Tanya Dolan again?
Gary   Yes. I'm working with Tanya on Tuesday. Then I'm
       meeting Sue Redman and James Barker on
       Wednesday, then I'm going to Paris.

Lilly	Really? Why are you going to Paris? On business?
Gary	No. I'm taking a break. I'm having two days off.
Lilly	Good idea. So, how are you travelling to Paris? Are you driving?
Gary	No. I'm taking the train – the Eurostar.
Lilly	Oh, right.
Gary	Then I'm staying in Paris for three nights.
Lilly	Great. So are you flying back to LA from Paris? Or …
Gary	No. I'm coming back to London on the train. Then I'm flying home on Saturday afternoon.
Lilly	OK.
Gary	I'm arriving in LA in the middle of the night. Just after midnight.
Lilly	Mmm. So, is it just one flight between LA and London?
Gary	No. I'm not flying direct. I'm going LA, New York, London. Then, on the flight home, I'm changing in Chicago.

▶▶ 81

Assistant	Hello.
Gary	Hi. I'd like to book two seats to Paris, please. For tomorrow.
Assistant	At what time?
Gary	At about five pm. I don't have a timetable.
Assistant	There's a train at seventeen fifteen. It arrives in Paris at twenty fifty-five, local time.
Gary	Right. OK, that's fine.
Assistant	Would you like to travel first class or standard class?
Gary	Standard.
Assistant	And would you like a single or a return ticket?
Gary	A round-trip, please.
Assistant	When would you like to come back?
Gary	I want to return on Saturday, but I don't know what time.
Assistant	Do you want to book the return trip now?
Gary	If I reserve a seat, can I change the reservation?
Assistant	With a standard fare, you can change or cancel the booking, yes.
Gary	OK. How much is the standard fare, then?
Assistant	One moment.

▶▶ 82

1 a single   2 a return   3 a timetable   4 local time
5 to return   6 to reserve   7 a reservation   8 a fare
9 standard

▶▶ 84

Customer	I'd like to book a ticket to Birmingham, please. A return.
Assistant	When do you want to leave?
Customer	July the thirtieth.
Assistant	The thirtieth?
Customer	Yes.
Assistant	At what time?
Customer	On the nine fifteen.
Assistant	In the morning?
Customer	Yes.
Assistant	And when are you coming back?

Customer	The day after. July the thirty-first. On the last train. I don't know what time it leaves.
Assistant	The last train's at … twenty fifteen.
Customer	OK. On the twenty fifteen, then.
Assistant	First or second class?
Customer	Second, please.
Assistant	That's … seventy-three pounds, please.

▶▶ 85

Colleague	Were you at the trade fair last week, Hanna? In India?
Hanna	Yes.
Colleague	Where was it? Delhi?
Hanna	Yeah.
Colleague	How was it? OK?
Hanna	It was very good, yeah.
Colleague	Was it big?
Hanna	Yeah. There were thousands of people.
Colleague	How many companies were there?
Hanna	Um … about four hundred, I think.
Colleague	Really?
Hanna	Yeah, it was big. I was surprised. I wasn't there last year. I was there two years ago, in Calcutta, and um … there weren't a lot of companies there. Only about a hundred.
Colleague	So this wasn't your first visit to India, then?
Hanna	No, my second.
Colleague	Right. Were you the only person there, from the company?
Hanna	No. Ingrid Werner was there, from the Frankfurt office. And Rafael and Maria, you know from, um …
Colleague	Oh, from Barcelona?
Hanna	Yeah.
Colleague	Were you all in the same hotel?
Hanna	We weren't in the same hotel, no. Um … but it was a good trip. Long, though.

▶▶ 87

Hanna	Martin, are you free for five minutes? Can we talk about your trip to Mexico?
Martin	Yeah, sure.
Hanna	So, how was it?
Martin	It was OK.
Hanna	When did you arrive?
Martin	Last Tuesday. Tuesday evening. I stayed Tuesday night, worked all day Wednesday and then travelled back Wednesday evening.
Hanna	Right. So where did you stay? What hotel were you in?
Martin	The Socorro Hotel. Near the office.
Hanna	Oh, yeah. It's good there.
Martin	Yeah. Um … Yes, so I presented the business plan on Wednesday morning.
Hanna	Right. Was Pedro happy?
Martin	Well … I wasn't sure at first. He didn't talk a lot after the presentation. We started at nine, I talked about the plan for thirty minutes, and … that was it. There were no questions. We finished at half past nine.

Hanna	Oh.
Martin	Hmm … I think he wanted to look at the figures in the report.
Hanna	Hmm.
Martin	He needed time to read it. Anyway, he phoned yesterday, with one or two questions. Just small points. And, er … he's happy. No problems.
Hanna	OK. That's fine, then. And did you talk about the cost of materials?
Martin	Yes. I talked to Miguel after the meeting. We discussed suppliers, as well, um … He's now talking to two new companies. I received an email this morning, saying he has a meeting with one company today, and one next Friday. So …
Hanna	OK. That's good. And did you visit the factory?
Martin	No. There was no time. So I didn't look at the new production line.
Hanna	Well, you're going again next month.
Martin	Yeah, that's right. I can see it then.
Hanna	OK. So, a good trip, then?
Martin	Yeah. So, how was your trip to Delhi?

▶▶ 88

1 He presented the business plan.
2 He talked about the cost of materials.
3 He discussed suppliers with Miguel.
4 He didn't visit the factory.
5 He didn't look at the new production line.

▶▶ 89

1 When did you arrive?
2 Where did you stay?
3 Did you talk about the cost of materials?
4 Did you visit the factory?

▶▶ 91

Hanna	Hi Steven.
Steven	Oh hi, Hanna. How are you?
Hanna	OK thanks. And you?
Steven	Not too bad. The first day back is never easy, but …
Hanna	Oh, of course, you're just back from holiday. I bet it was quiet in the office last week – I was in India, Martin was in Mexico, you were … where did you go?
Steven	Greece. Crete.
Hanna	Crete, OK. So how was it?
Steven	Fantastic. We really enjoyed it. We had two days in Athens, as well.
Hanna	Right. So your flight was to Athens?
Steven	Yeah. We flew to Athens. We stayed in a hotel there for … just one night. Then we took a ferry to Crete.
Hanna	The ferry left from Athens, then.
Steven	Yeah. It went direct to Chania in Crete, which was the town where we stayed, so …
Hanna	And did you stay in a hotel?

Steven	No, we rented an apartment – nothing special. We didn't spend a lot of time in it, really. We ate out every night. The nightlife was good – lots of restaurants and bars, and, er … the food was generally good … and it cost very little for a good meal.
Hanna	Mmm. So you enjoyed the food, and drank Greek wine, and …
Steven	Yeah. It was … all very relaxing.
Hanna	And how much of the island did you see? Did you travel around?
Steven	Yeah. We saw quite a few different places.
Hanna	So you rented a car and drove around, then …
Steven	No, no. We … we went on coach trips – organised trips – on a couple of days. And we travelled around by bus as well. You know, on … just on public buses. I don't speak a word of Greek, but … you just bought your ticket and … it was no problem.
Hanna	Sounds good.
Steven	We came back on Friday. So I had the weekend at home. And now … back to work! So how was your trip?

▶▶ 93

1 We had two days in Athens, as well.
2 We flew to Athens.
3 Then we took a ferry to Crete.
4 The ferry left from Athens, then.
5 It went direct to Chania in Crete.
6 We ate out every night.
7 It cost very little for a good meal.
8 So you enjoyed the food, and drank Greek wine … .
9 We saw quite a few different places.
10 So you rented a car and drove around, then.
11 You just bought your ticket and … it was no problem.
12 We came back on Friday.

▶▶ 95

1 gave   2 had   3 read   4 said   5 saw   6 sent
7 spoke   8 told   9 thought   10 wrote

▶▶ 96

A	Hello, APC Limited.
B	Hello, could I speak to André Thomas, please?
A	No, I'm afraid he's not here today.
B	Oh.
A	He's back tomorrow. Can I take a message?
B	Um … yes. Could you ask him to call me?
A	Sure.
B	My name's Jeanne Maire. J-E-A double N-E.
A	Sorry, could you say that again? I'm just … getting a pen.
B	Yeah. J-E-A double N-E.
A	J-E-A double N-E. Yeah.
B	Then Maire is M-A-I-R-E.
A	M-A-I-R-E. Right. And does he have your number?
B	Well, I'll give it to you. It's oh double one seven eight …
A	Oh one one seven eight. OK.
B	Double two seven six seven four one.

A Two two seven six seven four one.
B That's right.
A OK. I'll give him the message.
B Thanks very much. Bye.
A Bye.

▶▶ 99

1 I'll call back later.
2 I'll ask her to call you back.
3 I'll give her the message as soon as possible.

▶▶ 100

1 It's sunny.   2 It's raining.   3 It's cloudy.
4 It's snowing.   5 It's freezing.   6 It's windy.
7 It's foggy.   8 a thunderstorm

▶▶ 101

1 beautiful   2 miserable   3 warm   4 cool
5 minus one

▶▶ 102

Nigel   Well, it's a beautiful day.
Olivier Yeah, it's nice to see the sun. It rained nearly
         every day last week.
Nigel   Really?
Olivier Yeah. Not a very good start to the summer.
Nigel   Does it normally rain much here, in July?
Olivier No. You sometimes get one or two wet days.
         Or thunderstorms, sometimes. But, um ... anyway,
         the sun's shining today, that's the main thing.
Nigel   Yes. Ah ... The waiter's coming with our bottle of
         water.
Olivier Thank you. Would you like some?
Nigel   Yes, please.
Olivier So, is this your first visit to Marseille?
Nigel   No. I came here once before, about two years ago.
         In winter. It was ... it was quite warm, actually.
Olivier Yeah, winters are great here. Before, when I lived
         in Paris, I always hated winter. But here, it's, um ...
         if there's no wind, and the sun's out, you can wear
         a T-shirt. We get a cold wind, sometimes, called
         the Mistral. It blows down from the mountains ...
         from the Alps. But, um ... if it's sunny, and there's
         no wind, then it's ... it's quite warm.
Nigel   Well, my boss phoned me, from the UK office, half
         an hour ago. Apparently, it's raining there at the
         moment.
Olivier Oh dear.
Nigel   So, here's to our colleagues in London!
Olivier Yes. Cheers!
Nigel   Cheers!

▶▶ 104

1 further   2 better   3 worse

▶▶ 105

We all know that today companies want to spend less
on business travel. That means more businesspeople are
flying economy class. The advantage of economy class,
obviously, is the lower cost. The disadvantage is, you have
a smaller seat. If you want to work, it's not easy – your
table's very small, so you can't put papers on it. It's
difficult to use a laptop, etc.

So, we asked the question 'How can we make economy
class better for our business customers?'. And we think
we have the solution. So, that's what I'm going to talk
about now.

▶▶ 106

1   The safest way to travel is by plane.
2   The TGV is the fastest train in Europe.
3   Air France-KLM is the largest airline in Europe.
4   People often want to buy the cheapest tickets.
5   Some people want the most convenient way to travel.
6   Low-cost airlines often have the least expensive fares.
7   The best seats are in first class.

▶▶ 107

A What time do we get to Frankfurt? Quarter past?
B Um ... yes. Yes, we're on time, I think. The last time
   I took this flight it was about an hour late.
A Yeah? I don't usually fly. I normally go to Frankfurt on
   the train.
B From Paris?
A Yeah. It takes ... six and a half hours.
B Hmm.
A It's not a high-speed train.
B No. I drove last year, from Paris to Frankfurt. It took me
   ... six hours, I think.
A Right.
B No, the fastest way's by plane. Definitely.
A Oh yeah, I agree. I think the train's the most convenient
   way, though. There's more space, so you can work. You
   arrive right in the city centre.
B Oh, I'm not so sure. For me the most convenient way's
   the fastest way. I prefer to fly.
A Well, I suppose, for me, it's a question of cost, really.
   The train's cheaper.
B How much is it to Frankfurt?
A From Paris? It's about, um ... a hundred and eighty
   euros.
B Yeah. You're right. And that's cheaper than going by car.
   With fuel and running costs.
A Hmm. I don't like driving. I think it's the worst way to
   travel. For longer distances.
B Yes, that's true. When I drove to Frankfurt, I arrived at
   about ...

▶▶ 109

1   The flights to New York, London and Los Angeles aren't
     late. They're on time.
2   The flight to Tokyo is late. It's delayed by thirty minutes.
3   You can check in now for the flight to Los Angeles. The
     check-in is open.

4 You can't check in for the flight to London. The check-in is closed.
5 There's no flight to Singapore. It's cancelled.
6 For the flight to Los Angeles, go to gate D ten.
7 The passengers are getting on the plane to New York now. They're boarding.

▶▶ 110

Stewardess	Hello.
Passenger	Hello. Where did I put my ticket? Ah. There it is. Here you are.
Stewardess	Thank you. Do you have any ID?
Passenger	Sorry?
Stewardess	Do you have any identification? Your passport or an identity card …
Passenger	Oh yes. My passport. There you are.
Stewardess	Thanks. I'm afraid there are no window seats left. Is an aisle seat OK?
Passenger	Yes, that's fine.
Stewardess	The plane's quite full. The last flight was cancelled.
Passenger	Right. So is this flight on time?
Stewardess	Um … it's delayed about ten minutes. Do you have any luggage?
Passenger	Just one case.
Stewardess	A suitcase?
Passenger	No, it's just a briefcase. I'll take it as hand luggage.
Stewardess	OK. So you have no luggage to check in.
Passenger	No, I don't have any other bags.
Stewardess	OK, fine. Here's your boarding pass.
Passenger	Thank you.
Stewardess	We're boarding in … thirty-five minutes. Gate twelve B.
Passenger	Right. Um … are there any shops, after the security check?
Stewardess	No. There are some shops over there. Before you go through security.
Passenger	Oh, I see. OK, thank you.
Stewardess	You're welcome.

▶▶ 111

Kristi	So, where shall we meet?
Akio	Um … well, I can come to your office, or you can come here.
Kristi	Well, you came here last time, so … shall I come to Tokyo?
Akio	Yes, OK. Yeah, then you can meet our new design manager.
Kristi	Oh, yes. Good idea. OK, so let's meet in Tokyo.
Akio	OK. How many days do we need?
Kristi	Hmm … good question.
Akio	Shall we plan the meeting, first? Then we can decide when to meet, and how long we need …
Kristi	Yes, OK.
Akio	I wrote a list, this morning, of the things I'd like to look at with you.
Kristi	Right. Good.
Akio	So, um … well, shall I email it to you? Then you can look at it, and we can talk later.

Kristi	Yes, OK, good idea. Let's do that.
Akio	I'll send it now. And I'll call back, um … When shall I call you?
Kristi	Let's talk again in an hour.
Akio	OK, fine. Bye.
Kristi	Bye.

▶▶ 113

Akio	The most important job is the brochure – to start work on the sales brochure.
Kristi	Yes, I agree. I think we need to do that first. Um … but then, I think, before we check the prices, we need to choose the photos for the brochure. Hmm … I think that's more important.
Akio	Yes, you're right. That is urgent. The marketing people need those photos quickly.
Kristi	Yes. So, I think that …
Akio	And after that we can check the prices.
Kristi	Yes.
Akio	So that's all we need to do on the brochure. Um …
Kristi	Then, before we talk about new products, it's better if we look at the website design, because there's a lot of work to do on that.
Akio	Hmm. OK. Then, finally, we can talk about new products.
Kristi	Mmm, yes, if we have time. Let's do that last. It's not that urgent.
Akio	Yes, OK.
Kristi	So, how much time do we need to do all that?
Akio	Well, if we start quite early and work all day on the …

▶▶ 115

1 First of all, arrange a date for the meeting.
2 Then book a meeting room.
3 After that, prepare the agenda.
4 Finally, email the details to everybody.

▶▶ 116

1 A It's very important to check the dates.
   B Yes, I agree.
2 A The design of the brochure is a small job.
   B I'm not sure about that.
3 A I think you're the best person for the job.
   B I'm sorry, I don't agree.
4 A Shall we call to find out the latest figures?
   B That's a good idea.

▶▶ 117

Simon	So, when are you leaving for Tokyo?
Kristi	Um … next Wednesday. I'm leaving on Wednesday, coming back on Saturday.
Simon	Right. And you're going to meet Akio.
Kristi	Yes. We're going to work on the sales brochure. The Japanese brochure.
Simon	OK.
Kristi	Er … we're going to look at the website, as well.
Simon	Right. I wanted to ask you about that. What's the plan for the website, exactly?
Kristi	Well, I want to change the design. Um …

Simon Completely?
Kristi I think we need to make some big changes, yes.
Simon Why? What's the ... what's the aim?
Kristi Well, we need to make it easier to use. Um ... that's the main objective.
Simon Right.
Kristi And I want to improve the look, as well.
Simon Hmm. Are you going to show me the new site? Before you put it online?
Kristi Oh yes, sure.
Simon OK, good. When are you going to have it ready? What's your target date?
Kristi Well, our aim is to have the new site online this year ... before the end of the year. That's our goal. But, um ... I'm going to talk to Akio next week, and plan the project in detail. So I can send you a copy of the schedule after the meeting, if you want.
Simon Yes, OK, great. Right, well, have a good trip.
Kristi Thanks.

▶▶ 118

1 You're going to meet Akio.
2 I'm going to talk to Akio next week.
3 We're going to look at the website.
4 Are you going to show me the new site?
5 When are you going to have it ready?

▶▶ 119

(Rec = Receptionist)
Kristi Hello. I've got a reservation. Kristi Cortland.
Rec Ms Cortland ... a single room, for three nights?
Kristi That's right.
Rec OK. Could you fill in this form, please?
Kristi Sure. Have you got a pen?
Rec Yes. Here you are.
Kristi Thanks. Um ... It says 'company account number'. I haven't got the number. My company made the reservation, but, um, I don't ...
Rec It doesn't matter. You don't need to write that. Just put your name, address, passport number, and signature. That's fine.
Kristi OK.
Rec This is the card for your room.
Kristi To open the door?
Rec Yes. You just insert the card, and the door opens automatically.
Kristi Right. OK.
Rec It's room three one five, on the third floor.
Kristi Right.
Rec In the morning, breakfast is from six-thirty to ten.
Kristi From six-thirty. Right.
Rec The dining room's just over there.
Kristi OK.
Rec We've got twenty-four-hour room service. Just dial nine from your room.
Kristi Right.
Rec Would you like a wake-up call?
Kristi Um ... no. No, thanks.

Rec OK. And you've got a message from Mr Soga. He says he's coming to the hotel at seven forty-five.
Kristi Seven forty-five. Right. OK, thanks very much.
Rec You're welcome. Have a nice stay.
Kristi Thanks.

▶▶ 120

1 I've got a reservation.
2 Have you got a pen?
3 I haven't got the number.
4 We've got twenty-four-hour room service.
5 You've got a message from Mr Soga.

▶▶ 121

(Rec = Receptionist)
Kristi 'Morning. Could I check out, please?
Rec Certainly. Room three one five.
Kristi My company's paying the bill. I just have to pay the extras.
Rec OK. So, one phone call.
Kristi Yes. And some orange juice from the minibar.
Rec Yes. That's all. OK. So that's one thousand five hundred and fifty yen, please.
Kristi Can I pay by credit card?
Rec Of course.
Kristi Here you are.
Rec Thank you.

▶▶ 123

When I came here two years ago, I had one objective – stop losing money and start making a profit. My first goal was to improve business in the stores we had. We stopped opening new stores, we worked hard to increase sales and cut costs. And we did that quickly. Today, we have lower costs, higher sales, and a good profit margin. We're making money again.

Now, we can think about opening new stores. At the moment, we have no final target. Our aim is to open one new store at a time. It's better to progress slowly and make a profit, than grow fast and lose money.

Managers make their biggest mistakes when things are going well. I'm not saying we're doing well now. But we're not doing badly. We're on the right track, and we're aiming to stay on the right track. We're not going to try to run before we can walk.

▶▶ 125

1 At the moment, Toreador is doing quite well.
2 After Mr Clay joined the company, his people worked hard.
3 After Mr Clay joined the company, business improved quickly.
4 Mr Clay thinks it's better for businesses to grow slowly.

▶▶ 126

A So, how's business in Vienna?
B Um ... improving.
A Yeah?
B Yeah, slowly. It's um ... it's easier than last year.

A Yeah.

B We had a hard year, last year.

A Low sales?

B Well, we sold a lot of products. But, um ... nearly all low-margin goods.

A We had exactly the same situation in Dublin.

B Last year?

A Yeah. We made a profit – just.

B We lost money.

A Did you?

B Yeah. Not too much, but, um ...

A But this year, you're doing OK?

B Yeah, we're making money.

A That's good. We are. The good thing is, costs are lower this year, with the stronger euro.

B That's true, yeah. And they're getting lower. Of course, you're in the euro zone, in Ireland.

A That's right.

B So, do you just manage one store?

A Yeah, the Dublin branch. There is another one, in ...

▶▶ 129

A So how many T-shirts did we order?

B Um ... two thousand five hundred.

A Right. So it's quite a small order, then.

B Yeah. It's a new product, so we want to test it first.

A Sure. How many stores are we selling them in?

B Five.

A Right. And do you know the selling price?

B They're on sale at nine euros, in the stores. It's a cheap product.

A Hmm. Are we making much profit on them?

B On this order, forty percent.

A And what about bigger orders? How much discount can we get?

B Ten or fifteen percent more.

A So we can make a fifty, fifty-five percent profit margin on them?

B Yeah. And more, if they sell well. I think we can get a maximum twenty percent discount on really big orders.

A Is there much demand at the moment? That's the question. Do many people want to buy T-shirts in winter?

B Well, people buy them to wear under sweaters and shirts ...

▶▶ 132

1

Assistant Do you need any help?

Customer Yes, how much is this T-shirt? I can't find the price on it.

Assistant Er ... Let's have a look. ... Is that it, there? Yes. Thirteen pounds.

Customer Oh right. OK. Thank you.

2

Customer Excuse me. I'm just looking at these shoes. I'm a size forty-five, European size. What's that in a UK size? Do you know?

Assistant UK size, that's a ... ten-and-a-half.

Customer Right. Could I try them in a ten-and-a-half, then, please?

Assistant Yes, I'll go and get you a pair.

Customer Thanks.

3

Assistant Can I help you?

Customer Yes, I'd like to look at a watch, if I can, please.

Assistant Sure.

Customer It's that one there, at the back.

Assistant This one here?

Customer Yes, that's it.

Assistant There you are.

Customer Thanks. So it's ninety-nine fifty?

Assistant Ninety-nine pounds fifty, that's right. Guaranteed for two years.

4

Assistant Hello.

Customer Hello. Could I have one of those, please?

Assistant One of these, here? The bracelets?

Customer Yes.

Assistant What colour would you like? There's blue, pink ... yellow. Um ... I think we've got them in green, as well.

Customer Um ...

Assistant Is it a present?

Customer Yeah. It's not for me!

Assistant That's what they all say!

Customer It's for my daughter. She's thirteen. Um ...

Assistant The pink ones are nice.

Customer I'll have a pink one, then, please. Thank you.

5

Assistant That's thirty-nine pounds ninety, please.

Customer Can I pay with this credit card?

Assistant Yes, we accept those. That's fine.

Customer Here you are.

Assistant Thanks. If you could just sign here. ... Thanks.

▶▶ 134

1 I don't often go shopping for clothes but when I go, I buy quite a lot. I usually know what I want before I go. So I just buy what I need, and come back as soon as I have everything. And I try to go when it's quiet. I hate shopping when it's busy.

2 I love shopping ... especially for clothes. Even if it's only window shopping. I don't think I spend too much on clothes. I don't buy lots of things and then never wear them, like some people. But I can understand why people do that.

Acknowledgements

The authors would like to acknowledge above all the significant contribution to the course made by Nathalie and Aimy Ibbotson, and Evgenia Miassoedova. They were a constant source of support and ideas at all stages of the project and displayed remarkable patience!

Thanks also to: Will Capel for believing in the project and for his advice and expertise during the critical early stages of development, Sally Searby for her encouragement and commitment to getting the best out of the course, Clare Abbott for her excellent editorial input – especially in guiding the material through key improvements to the concept and methodology, Elin Jones for her valuable editorial advice, ideas and positive support – much appreciated during the intense phase of writing the first level, and Chris Capper for his helpful input on the early units. A big thanks to our editor Nick Robinson, whose positive energy, ideas and feel for the material have been instrumental in shaping the second level. And a special thanks to our copy editor Fran Banks, for giving *Business Start-up* the benefit of her expertise, eagle eyes and extremely hard work.

We would also like to thank the many reviewers who have offered valuable comments on the material at various stages of development, including Alex Case, Helen Forrest, Radoslaw Lewandowski, Rosemary Richey and Robert Szulc.

The publisher would like to thank the following for permission to reproduce photographs:

Alamy for pp. 52 (a l & b r), 85 (b r) & 87 (boots and t-shirt); Acestock Ltd for p. 34 (4 & 5); Arcaid for p. 85 (b r); Black Star for p. 20 (b); Peter Bowater for p. 61 (r); Car Photos for pp. 24 (r) & 48 (l); Imageshop - Zefa Visual Media Ltd for pp. 52 (b l) & 60 (tr); imagestopshop for p.18 (3); Imagestate for p. 16 (tr); Andre Jenny for p.16 (l); Richard Levine for p. 28 (b); Steven May for pp. 28 (t) & 56 (t); Medioimages for pp. 52 (d) & 61 (l); Motoring Picture Library for p. 64 (t); Charlie Newham for pp. 46/47(t); David Paterson for p. 18 (5); plainpicture for p. 31; Rubberball for pp. 52 (e), 58 (tm), & 82 (2); David Sanger Photography for p. 52 (c); SCPhotos for p. 28 (m); Stockbyte for p. 52 (b m); South West Images Scotland for pp. 34 (1) & 52 (a r); David Wall for p. 39 (inset); David Young-Wolff, Alvey & Towers for p. 17, 36 (a); Aviation images for p. 60 (tl); Corbis for pp. 10 (br), 14, 29, 34 (2), 34 (7), 42, 56 (b), 58 (tl), 72 (b), 75, 82 (1 & 3), 85 (a r & c l) & 87 (Rolex & earrings); Courtesy of easyJet for p. 62; Getty Images for pp. 18 (1, 2 & 4), 20 (t), 21, 22 (4), 37, 41 (3), 58 (tr) & 59; Imagestate for pp. 22 (5), 36 (d) & 72(t); istockphoto.com for pp. 14 (br), 27 (bl) & 47 (tr); Photolibrary.com for pp. 34 (6), 50 (t) & 63 (l); Punchstock for pp. 22 (7), 24 (l) & 44; Bananastock for pp. 7(bl & tr) & 7(bm); Blend Images for pp. 34 (3) & 47(t); Brand X Pictures for pp. 7 (tl) & 41 (2); Corbis for pp. 19 & 36 (c);

Creatas for pp. 36 (e), 41 (1) & 66 (r); Digital Vision for p. 18 (6); Imageshop - Zefa Visual Media Ltd for pp. 50 (br) & 85 (mr); Imagesource for p. 63 (r) IT Stock; Courtesy of Siemens for p. 12 (l); Superstock for pp. 16 (br), 22 (2), 32, 70, 74 & 85 (a l, b l, c r); TIPS Images for p. 36 (b); Topfoto for p. 76; Zefa Visual Media Ltd for pp. 22 (1), 82 (4) & 85 (br).

The authors and publishers are grateful to the following for permission to use copyright material in *Business Start-up 1*. While every effort has been made, it has not been possible to identify the sources of all the material used and in such cases the publishers would welcome information from the copyright owners:

The IBM logo on p. 6 with permission of IBM; the UPS logo on p. 6 with permission of UPS; the Volkswagen logo on p. 6 with permission of Volkswagen; the AOL logo on p. 6 with permission of AOL; the GEC logo on p. 6 with permission of the General Electric Company; the TDK logo on p. 6 with permission of TDK; for the table on p. 16. 'The Big Mac index' from *The Economist*, 18 December, 2004, © The Economist Newspaper Limited; the Amazon logo http://www.amazon.co.uk on p. 28 with permission of Amazon; the easyJet logo http://www.easyJet.com on p. 28 with permission of easyJet Airline Co. Ltd; the iTunes logo on p. 28 with permission of Apple Computer, Inc; for the jacket covers on p. 40, *Fishing For Dummies* by Peter Kaminsky. Copyright © 1997 by Wiley Publishing, Inc. All rights reserved. Reproduced here by permission of the publisher. For Dummies is a registered trademark of Wiley Publishing Inc; *Skiing For Dummies* by Allen St. John. Copyright © 1999 IDG Books Worldwide, Inc. All rights reserved. Reproduced here by permission of the publisher. For Dummies is a registered trademark of Wiley Publishing Inc;

Commissioned Photography by Gareth Boden pp. 6, 7(br), 8, 22(3, 6 & r), 30, 38/39(t), 66(l), 68, 71.

Cover images by (the graph) Alamy: (the stopwatch) Corbis.

Picture Research by Kevin Brown

Book design by Pentacor**big**